The

Guide to Small Business Marketing

The
facebook®
Guide to Small
Business Marketing

by Ramon Ray

WILEY

John Wiley & Sons, Inc.

The Facebook® Guide to Small Business Marketing

Published by
John Wiley & Sons, Inc.
10475 Crosspoint Blvd.
Indianapolis, IN 46256
www.wiley.com

Published simultaneously in Canada

ISBN: 978-0-470-87520-9 *5OHG 396G 03/13*

Manufactured in the United States of America

10 9 8 7 6 5 4 3 2 1

For general information on our other products and services or to obtain technical support, please contact our Customer Care Department within the U.S. at (877) 762-2974, outside the U.S. at (317) 572-3993 or fax (317) 572-4002.

Wiley publishes in a variety of print and electronic formats and by print-on-demand. Some material included with standard print versions of this book may not be included in e-books or in print-on-demand. If this book refers to media such as a CD or DVD that is not included in the version you purchased, you may download this material at http://booksupport.wiley.com. For more information about Wiley products, visit www.wiley.com.

Library of Congress Control Number: 2010941209

WILEY

About the Author

Ramon Ray (www.ramonray.com) is a technology evangelist who is passionate about helping small businesses grow using technology as a strategic asset. He is also regional development director, NY for Infusionsoft (a sales and marketing software company). Ramon is a journalist, event producer, speaker, author, and editor of smallbiztechnology.com. His previous two books include *Technology Solutions for Growing Businesses* (AMACOM Books, 2003) and *Technology Resources for Growing Businesses* (2011).

As a journalist and writer, Ramon has written thousands of articles (product reviews, interviews, and more) about technology for small businesses. His work appears on smallbiztechnology.com and also on allbusiness.com, entrepreneur.com, openforum.com, blackenterprise.com, and more.

Hundreds of small business owners have attended his events, including the Small Business Summit (www.smallbiztechsummit.com), Small Business Technology Tour (www.smallbiztechtour.com), and Small Business Influencer Awards (http://influencers.smallbiztrends.com).

Ramon is a speaker whose audiences routinely use the words *informative* and *energized* when describing his content and speaking style. Ramon has spoken at the Inc. 500, OPEN Forum at Consumer Electronics Show with Guy Kawasaki, Black Enterprise Entrepreneur's Conference & Expo, New York Expo, Infusionsoncon, and many other events.

Ramon is not just a technology writer. As a former small-business technology consultant, he has years of hands-on experience in building networks, installing software, upgrading computers, and supporting the technology that small businesses use daily.

Ramon is often quoted in the media, including in *Crain's New York*, the *New York Times*, the *Wall Street Journal*, the *San Francisco Chronicle*, and others.

Credits

Acquisitions Editor
Aaron Black

Project Editor
Kristin Vorce

Technical Editor
Paul Hammond

Senior Copy Editor
Kim Heusel

Editorial Director
Robyn Siesky

Business Manager
Amy Knies

Senior Marketing Manager
Sandy Smith

Vice President and Executive Group
Publisher
Richard Swadley

Vice President and Executive Publisher
Barry Pruett

Project Coordinator
Katie Crocker

Graphics and Production Specialists
Jennifer Henry
Jennifer Mayberry

Quality Control Technician
Lauren Mandelbaum

Proofreading and Indexing
Linda Seifert
Valerie Haynes Perry

*To my family — Ronnie (wife), Timothy (son), Charity (daughter),
Clabe (father — deceased 1998), Olivia (mother),
Clalin (sister), and Joanna (sister).*

*To the 30 million small businesses who continue to struggle with
acquiring new customers and keeping the ones they have.*

Acknowledgments

I would like to deeply thank Carolyn Crummey (VirTasktic) for her supreme collaboration to bring this book to fruition (hundreds of e-mails and more). Thanks to Laura Leites (L2 Event Production) and Pierre DeBois (Zimana) for their help and contributions toward this book's production and research.

contents at a glance C

contents

Chapter 4
Making Money on Facebook... 71

Contents

Contents

When I wake up in the morning, I first think, "What can I do to build deeper relationships with the customers I have?" And second, "What can I do to build relationships with new customers?" There are many ways to do this, such as being nice, speaking at events, nurturing referrals, and so much more. Many of the old ways of building relationships still work, but compared to digital communication, those ways are often slow and hard to measure.

Digital communication (blogs, websites, e-mail newsletters, online advertising, and so on) enables you to reach new and current customers faster — to track their responses to your communications, to enable them to forward your message to others — all with a few clicks of the mouse.

With the advent of social media, digital communication capabilities have grown exponentially. Not only can businesses communicate directly with their audiences, but audiences can more easily communicate with businesses, and audiences (customers and potential customers) can communicate with each other about businesses, brands, products, services, or marketplaces.

When small business owners look for new customers, the Internet is the best option — it's better than print, TV, radio, Yellow Pages, billboards, and so on. The Internet provides a variety of ad options small businesses can consider, such as search engine advertisements, banner advertisements, mobile advertisements, and social media. But if I had to pick one place for advertising online, it would be Facebook. It has the broadest range of options. Facebook is perfect for small businesses on a low budget that are just testing the waters or businesses with a much larger budget and more experience. Facebook allows you to reach a broad audience or be very selective and target a specific audience, making it an effective way to reach potential customers and beyond.

With approximately 1 billion profiles, Facebook has just about everyone. If you're looking for a business customer, a retired uncle, a military veteran, a stay-at-home mom, a high school teacher, or your "average" consumer, you'll find them all on Facebook.

As you'll see in this book, Facebook gives you a variety of free tools to engage with your audience (through great content — posts, photos, video, and more), interact with customers (Check-in Deals), voting, interactive apps, advertising, and so much more.

This book will help you strategically use Facebook as a powerful communications tool. Maybe you just want to start by posting a relevant message or two. Maybe you want to get fancy and include a video and photo. How about taking the training wheels off and building a better Facebook Page for your business, product, or service? What about customizing this Page with some cool and useful apps? Getting comfortable? It might be time to purchase advertising on Facebook and drive local traffic to your local retail store.

This book also covers creating Facebook events, driving traffic to your website through Facebook, and catching media attention. And I think one of the best parts of the book is the real-world examples from successful small businesses.

John Wanamaker, a famous advertising executive, once said, "I know half my advertising is wasted; I'm just not sure which half." Using Facebook is much better than print advertising to precisely reach the right customers, measure your return on investment and their engagement with your product or service, and ultimately, make a sale.

You're working with customers, hiring employees, and doing so many other things to manage your business day to day while still looking toward the future. Although customer acquisition and development are not easy, using Facebook can make it a lot easier.

chapter 1

Timeline | Info | Photos | Notes

Learning Facebook Basics

Can you remember what life was like before Facebook? You sent e-mails to friends. Maybe you participated in online chats and you might (just might) have watched some online video. However, to really keep up with your friends, family, customers, and colleagues, you talked to them on the phone or visited them face to face. Facebook and other social networks have changed all that. You now get status updates the moment your daughter gets her first job and you see photos of your customers using one of your products. This is the power of Facebook and the power of social media: It brings people together online to discuss common interests. This chapter explains what social media and Facebook are all about.

The Power of "Social" in Social Media

Although direct e-mail and flyers in the Sunday newspaper are still great ways to attract new customers or engage with the ones you have, social media enables marketers (that's you) to work in a new dimension.

With social media marketing, you are able to do more than just sell your product — you can leverage the power of your customers to tell others about your products, services, or brand within the context of their social networks. Social media is also powerful because you can find customers who are already talking about your specific product or company or about something related to your industry.

According to a June 2011 blog post by ClickZ, social media is a proven success for marketing very "sexy" products, especially those that are focused on consumers. When companies offer money or discounts to customers in exchange for "liking" them on Facebook, many of their customers (and new customers) sign up for the offer (see Figure 1.1). The challenge has been for companies who are also trying to attract new customers and get them to take deeper action, such as signing up for a new bank account or buying a product.

However, companies are finding that social media is indeed a very powerful way to get people to encourage others to take action. For example, a ClickZ blog post reports that Discover Card created a social media referral program that rewarded card holders $50 for each friend they got to become a card holder. And Zecco Trading, an online investing site, offered its customers $75 for every friend who opened and funded a new Zecco Trading account. The company realized a big increase in new accounts by offering incentives.

Social media is an explosively powerful way to get customers to influence their friends to take favorable action toward your brand, product, or service. It just takes creativity and thinking through who to best use on Facebook to influence those decisions.

 Half the success in getting the most out of Facebook is knowing how to use it. The other half is knowing what creative ways you can use to engage your audience to take profitable action.

So do you see why Facebook can be so powerful? Facebook has a billion users, all connected in one way or another. Diving into this swimming pool of connectivity means that your customers and potential customers can engage with your brand through photos, coupons, videos, surveys, polls, and so many other things.

1.1 Businesses offer discounts to consumers for liking their Facebook Pages.

Content Is King and Customer Engagement Is Queen

Before diving into Facebook, you should understand the importance of content and customer engagement. Creating high-quality content is one of the key aspects of using social networks to engage your audience.

People, be they business owners, stay-at-home moms, soccer dads, corporate lawyers, or cooks at local restaurants, want online content. They either want to be entertained (Hulu, YouTube) or they want to be informed (Wikipedia, HowStuffWorks.com).

People's interests span a wide range of topics — the location of the nearest restaurant, how to get rid of a nagging headache, intricacies of real estate law, and anything else relevant to their business or personal lives. This is why, in regard to your own business, content is so important. People on Facebook are looking for information, not just a product to buy. It is important that you have the information they want so that when they are ready to buy, they will associate that found information with the product that you are selling.

People (and remember, *people* run businesses and buy business products for their businesses) are not just looking for content. They also like to be engaged. They want to comment on your posts, send you a video of them using your product, take a survey, and so on. All these things and more are engagement.

Almost 1 billion people are on Facebook — this is clear evidence that people want content (which Facebook helps produce) and engagement with each other (which Facebook also helps facilitate).

It is important to sell and market your products and services, but it is equally (and maybe even more) important to create valuable content so that customers can not only find you online but also can engage and interact with you (see Figure 1.2).

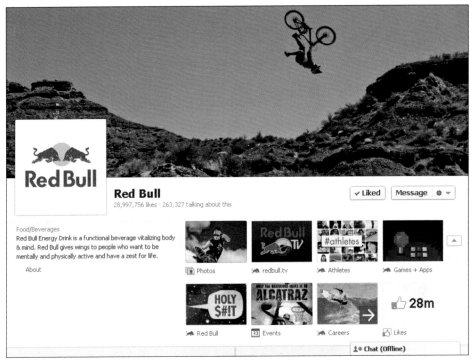

1.2 Red Bull's Facebook fans not only get information about its products but also are asked to engage in polls and share their experiences with the company and other followers.

What Is Facebook?

Most people think they know what Facebook is, and for the most part they're right. However, many people use Facebook and really have no clue what it is or what it can do for them. The rest of this chapter reviews some of Facebook's key features. You explore why the world (or the almost 1 billion people in the world on Facebook) is so enamored with Facebook. You then learn why people are excited about using Facebook for business.

Why are individuals using Facebook?

Facebook is a platform that enables users to share information about themselves with friends. *Friends* are the individuals within the Facebook community to whom you give permission to connect and share information. This information, shared through status updates, enables friends and those who "like" your Pages to receive updates from you and for you to share information about yourself. Status updates appear when you post to your Facebook Timeline — all those in your community (who have liked your Page or are your friend) see your updates.

You can do more than just post messages on your Facebook Timeline — Facebook enables you to use tools for event notifications, videos, photos, and more.

An ecosystem of independent software developers has grown to create third-party applications for Facebook. These applications take Facebook's platform and layer games, utilities, and collaboration tools on top of it, allowing users to do even more with Facebook.

Why are small businesses using Facebook?

The goal of any business — including yours — is to find where your customers are and market to them to ultimately sell more of your product or service. With over 60 percent of the U.S. population on Facebook, nearly every business is now looking at the social network as a new medium to reach current and potential customers.

Facebook is an ideal platform to engage with your current customers and advertise to find new customers. I discuss more on this later.

By leveraging the same tools available for consumers and creating their own applications, businesses can complement their existing online marketing with the power of Facebook.

Facebook Statistics

These numbers give you an idea of the breadth and scope of Facebook. (You can find the most updated statistics at http://newsroom.fb.com).

- Facebook has 1 billion monthly active users as of October 2012.
- Approximately 81 percent of monthly active users are outside the United States and Canada.
- Facebook had 584 million daily active users on average in September 2012.
- There were 604 million monthly active users who used Facebook mobile products as of September 30, 2012.
- An average of 3.2 billion likes and comments were generated by Facebook users per day during the first quarter of 2012.
- Facebook is available in more than 70 languages.

Maybe you are using Eventbrite to manage your customer appreciation events. Now you can give customers an option to register through Facebook. Maybe your customers are not thrilled about signing up for a traditional e-mail newsletter — they can now get your updates through Facebook.

Are you starting to understand why 1 billion people are on Facebook and how your business can benefit?

Because Facebook has almost a billion users and dozens of groups and apps per person, it's important that you work to bring your brand to Facebook and Facebook to your brand. Consider a fictional local florist who owns a flower shop in the suburbs. While many customers talk about this florist using traditional word of mouth, many also share pictures of her floral arrangements on a variety of online forums, including Facebook. Most of all, her customers are on Facebook, and it's therefore essential that she create a corporate Page to engage with customers, letting them comment and share their experiences. In her flower shop, she could post a sign by the cash register that says "Post photos of your favorite flower to our Facebook Page this week for a chance to win a free floral arrangement." This is bringing Facebook to your brand.

Many businesses are still experimenting with the results of their efforts with social media in general. Having said that, studies indicate that approximately 40 percent of small businesses use social media.

But most understand that a lot is at stake if no effort is exerted. According to eMarketers, the percentage of Internet users who use social media is growing, expecting to reach 67 percent by 2013. Experian's benchmark and trend report, *The 2011 Digital Marketer,* noted that over 70 percent of adults compare prices online before making a purchase and 17 percent of adults search social networking sites before buying something. These numbers indicate more than public acceptance of social media — they also mean that your online presence for your business will make or break a sales decision in the eyes of your customer. And with Facebook being a leading social media platform, developing a Facebook business presence is certainly essential.

Quote, Unquote: Success with Facebook

If you are still unsure about how Facebook can help your business, here are some Facebook comments from small-business owners in the United States who have used the social network successfully:

"I am the president of Rosebay Development Partners, which is a communications consulting firm. We began using Facebook last year to augment messaging and branding for our clients. The results have been nothing short of incredible! There is no other web medium where a company can have such an intimate conversation with a client or a potential client."

— Jay Wilson, Birmingham, Alabama

"I have always taken pics of my family. Friends. Daughter. Everything! Because of Facebook, everyone noticed. Now I have a very successful and exciting small photography business! I don't answer a single phone — I conduct *all* of my business through Facebook — chat, messaging, comments, etc. Because of that, I can keep business and evening family time separated."

— Shannon Sweeney Fulton, Camden, Tennessee

chapter 2

Designing a Business Page

Your Facebook business Page is one of the most important assets you have in successfully marketing your business. You can drive lots of visitors to your Facebook Page and update your status frequently, but if you have not taken the time to create a well-designed Page, all these things are useless.

Designing a successful Facebook Page is deceptively easy. Any business owner can create a Facebook Page in less time than it takes to drink a cup of tea, but it takes a bit of thought, planning, and technical tinkering to make your Facebook Page just right for you and your business and encourage visitors to take the action you want. This chapter helps you design a great Facebook Page.

Facebook Business Pages versus Traditional Websites

My friend Navin Ganeshan, chief product strategist at online marketing and web host company Network Solutions, has his finger on the pulse of how small business owners can successfully build their businesses online. In this chapter, Navin shares his insight.

As you start creating your Facebook business Page, it is likely to remind you of the process of designing a website. You face the same considerations regarding the logo, colors, and links, and you need to adhere to some of the same do's and don'ts of design and content. And yes, you'll most likely even experience the same writer's block.

In the days before Facebook (hard to imagine, I know), small-business websites took on the full burden of creating a compelling presence, listing all the information that visitors wanted to see and serving as the place for visitors to interact with your business by commenting, sharing, and reviewing.

This was rarely done well. It took considerable effort from the business owner to create a welcoming experience that invited participation. Also, visitors had little incentive for participating, primarily because the experience lacked social context. Enter Facebook, which provides that social context by sharing your likes, comments, visits, and activities with your friends, and vice versa.

Your website and your Facebook Page are subtly differentiated in function, as outlined in Table 2.1. Think of your website as where you really want to convey the full breadth and depth of your business using your own unique style and descriptive content about your services. Your Facebook Page is primarily the point of interaction between you and your customers, where you speak to them directly and they talk back to you about your product or service.

While a Facebook business Page has strengths and limitations, ultimately, how you use it depends on your needs, the nature of your business, and your willingness to invest time. Some businesses configure their Page to support everything from product sales to customer service request tracking.

Table 2.1 Business Website and Facebook Business Page: The Subtle Differences

Website	Facebook
You have full creative control	You have limited control
Focus on presentation	Focus on interaction
Visitors expect uniqueness	Visitors expect uniqueness, but in a familiar context
Frequent content updates needed	Content changes in real time

Facebook Redesigns

In early 2011, Facebook made some high-profile changes to the layout and technology behind its business Pages. The most important of these was a switch from a proprietary technology called Facebook Markup Language (FBML) to a more flexible IFRAME layout. The IFRAME layout enables you to embed a website element (such as a picture, graphic, or other element) more easily inside another web page. The change was made as part of a move to HTML5, an update of the basic web coding format being rolled out slowly to improve compatibility with media tags and mobile devices.

The most significant change to business Pages has been the mandatory conversion to the Timeline format. The Timeline shows a chronological, diary-like, display of all that's happened on your Facebook Page. You can see what's happening now or last year or three years ago. With this change comes an entirely new anatomy of the business Page and how information is viewed and shared.

The largest change, aesthetically, is the addition of the cover photo in place of the photo strip. Instead of using a series of photos that constantly change (as the photo strip did) to identify and describe your business on your Page, the cover photo gives you a much larger space to use a dedicated image to convey your brand or image to visitors.

Timeline also changes the way your Page content is viewed. The different areas of content on your profile Page are now organized using links located beneath your cover photo instead of tabs at the top. These are referred to as *views and apps*. Despite the change, many people still routinely refer to the individual Pages as *tabs*. Photos, Likes, Events, and custom apps that you create for your business Page, such as a Welcome Page, are examples of the types of links that appear within the views and apps section of your Page.

Many new tools were added with Timeline as well, including pinned posts, starred or hidden stories, and milestones. Each of these tools allows you different ways of highlighting stories on your Page and managing how they appear to your visitors.

Here are the key components of the Facebook Timeline:

- **Cover photo.** This is a dedicated image of your brand, product, or service.

- **Profile picture.** This is the smaller image that appears below your cover photo. This image represents your company and appears as a thumbnail in News Feed stories, ads, and Sponsored Stories, so it should be an image that your followers can easily associate with you, such as a logo. I cover customizing your profile picture later in this chapter.

- **Views and apps.** These are the boxes that appear below your cover photo and link to your photos, events, and custom apps (see Figure 2.1).

Profile picture   Cover photo

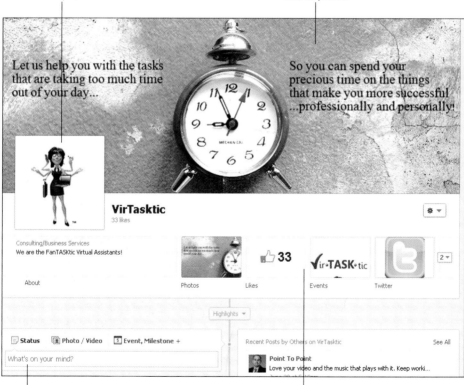

Composer   Views and apps

2.1 The cover photo, profile picture, composer, and views and apps boxes in the Timeline.

- **Composer.** The composer is the open box on your Page where you can post updates and photos, ask questions, or enter milestones. Posting regularly on your Page increases your reach to your audience and encourages engagement.

- **Pinned post.** You can pin, or anchor, a story so it appears at the top of your Page by using the Story Edit button and clicking Pin to Top (see Figure 2.2). The story will remain at the top of your Page for up to seven days.

- **Star and hide stories.** This function allows you to highlight, or star, important stories that appear on your Page or to hide stories that are not as engaging or relevant.

- **Milestones.** You can create milestones that define key moments of your business, such as when you opened, so they appear on your Timeline.

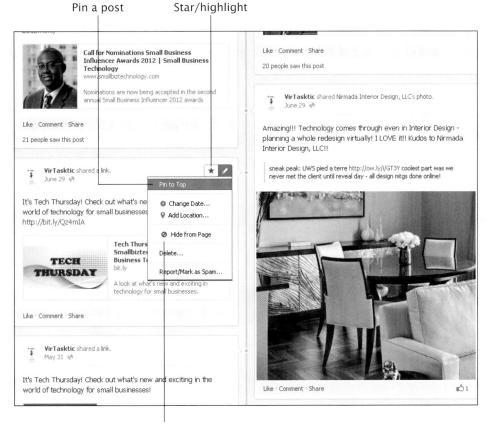

2.2 You can pin posts, star stories, or hide stories.

To see a full, detailed outline of all of the components of Timeline and the layout features, visit http://ads.ak.facebook.com/ads/FacebookAds/Pages_Product_Guide_022712.pdf.

Because the changes make it easier to achieve a higher level of sophistication and visual effects, you can choose to design your own Page, as explained in this chapter, or choose to use one of the many Facebook Page design tools that have popped up (several with free versions) that make it much easier to get started. The choice is yours, and this chapter gives you information about each of the choices so you can get your Page up and running in no time.

Designing Your Basic Facebook Page

Once you decide that you are going to create a Facebook Page for your business, you can use a number of options to design your Page and publish it on Facebook. In this section, I explain the basic steps of creating and designing a Page using the standard Facebook tools. Though these tools are available to everyone and are quite simple, they only enable you to create a very basic Facebook Page without many bells or whistles. Creating a Page with these tools is a nice baby step for those who want to set up something simple or establish a basic presence that they will update later with additional designs and tools.

You must follow some basic steps to get your Page up and running in Facebook, which I outline in the following sections.

Creating a Facebook login

You more than likely already have a functioning Facebook login and may have a business Page already in existence. If not, you need to set this up before continuing. To set up a Facebook account, follow these steps:

1. **Go to www.facebook.com.** On the right-hand side of the website you see Sign Up.

2. **Complete all the fields in the Sign Up boxes and then click Sign Up.** You have now created a Facebook account.

NOTE You will notice that under the Sign Up boxes on the Facebook home Page there is a link to Create a Page for a celebrity, band, or business. By using this link, you can create a business Page without having a personal Facebook account. I strongly suggest that you do not create your Page this way, but instead create a personal account first to link to your business Page. By doing this, you will have better control and additional privacy settings available for your Page.

Creating a business Page

Once you have a personal Facebook account, click the Create a Page link at the bottom of your Account Settings page or go to www.facebook.com/pages/create.php (see Figure 2.3).

Create a Page option

2.3 The option to create a Page is found under Account Settings on your personal Facebook Page.

You can create a number of different types of Pages, including Local Business or Place; Company, Organization, or Institution; Brand or Product; and a few others. Choose the Page type that most closely reflects your type of business. For example, if you are a retail business or restaurant and have an actual business location, choose Local Business or Place. If you provide consulting or business services and work from your home or a private office, then you would most likely want to choose Company, Organization, or Institution. Think carefully about what kind of organization you want to display. Some Pages, depending on the type, have limited features while others do not, which can require some unorthodox management headaches when your followers grow significantly. For example, a local business Page has an address while a company, organization, or institution Page does not.

Once you've chosen the type of Page to create, you need to specify the name of the Page, which should be your business name. After you design your main Page, you can add additional views and apps to your Page, which allows you to highlight different aspects of your business such as products, photos, and services.

Customizing Page content

Your Page content is the meat and potatoes of your business Page. Customizing Page content can feel like adding a fresh coat of paint and sprucing up the hand rails of an old house in that the details become important when considered together. Some Page elements are within your control from a design perspective while others are not, but they all work together as your overall business presence (see Figure 2.4).

Ensure you have a good and high-resolution photo that shows the business at work. Add a summary that tells users a little information about your organization, brand, or product. It's important that you relay enough information so that people know who you are, what you do, and what you offer, but not so much information that your visitors are overwhelmed. Customizing your Page and adding content is very easy and you should focus on the following elements.

Profile picture   Cover photo

Composer   Timeline   Post

2.4 The basic elements of a Facebook business Page.

Profile picture

Your profile picture typically represents your business logo. Use an image that scales well from 180×180 to 32×32 pixels, as this image follows your business as a thumbnail image in News Feeds, ads, and Sponsored Stories. This is usually the first element you want to customize because nothing is more uninviting to visitors than a business Page without a profile picture (see Figure 2.5).

NOTE You only need to add a profile picture if you didn't upload an image during Page creation.

2.5 The default Facebook business Page.

Adding a profile picture is quick and simple and can be done by following these steps:

1. **When your new Page is launched, you are on the Get Started page where you are prompted to Add an Image for your profile picture.** Click the Upload an Image link.

2. **A pop-up box prompts you to click the Choose File.** Click Choose File and find the file you want to use as the profile picture on your computer.

3. **Double-click on the file and the image will upload right away.** After the file is uploaded, it automatically appears as your profile picture. (Note: If you don't like the picture as it appears, you have to edit it outside of Facebook so it fits the dimensions allowed and then reupload the file.)

If you have uploaded an image as your profile picture, but you want to change it, it is still very simple but the steps are slightly different:

1. **Hover your mouse over the existing profile photo.**

2. **Click Edit Profile Picture.**

3. **If you want to use an existing file, click Choose from Photos and you will go to your photo albums.** Choose the photo you want to use and click Make Profile Picture for Page.

4. **To add a new file, click Upload Photo or Take Photo.** You are prompted to either choose a file from a location on your computer or to take a picture to add. (Note: You must have a webcam on your computer to take a picture to add.) After you take a picture with your webcam, click Save Picture.

5. **After you choose the file you want to add, it automatically becomes your new profile picture.**

Once again, make sure that the picture you choose for you profile picture is a good representation of your business and the image you want to portray to your Facebook following.

Business information

When creating your Page, you want to provide all the basic information about your business along with a description of your products or services. During the Page setup process you provide general information about your Page, but once it's set up you'll want to add more in-depth information. You can do that by following these steps:

1. **Open the Admin Panel on the top right of your business Page and click Edit Page.**

2. **Click the Admin Panel, then click Update Info from the drop-down list to view Basic Information.** A new Page appears that includes sections for you to complete, including Name, Start Date, Start Type, Address, About, Description, Mission, Awards, Products, Email, Phone, and Website (see Figure 2.6). Complete each of these fields with as much information as you can provide. (Note: You can go back any time and change this information.)

3. **Click Save Changes on the bottom of the Page to save your information.**

Again, tailor your information to fit your type of business and what information you want available to your followers. For example, if you're a car mechanic, include what types of car repairs you can do.

2.6 Complete all the information about your business Page so that those that visit understand who you are and what you do.

Timeline posts

When you build your Facebook business Page, keep in mind what should be reflected on your Timeline. The Timeline is where your updates and posts are displayed. You can adjust who can post on your Timeline and add moderation filters through the Manage Permissions page (just above the Basic Information option).

Once visitors click the Like button on your Page, they then have the ability to see your Timeline posts in their News Feed. Timeline posts should be used to convey information about your company to your followers. For example, if you are a retail location and you have a new product you are introducing, create a Timeline post about the product. To create a Timeline post, follow these steps (see Figure 2.7):

2.7 Posting updates and pictures to your Timeline keeps followers informed on what's happening in your business and encourages interaction.

1. **Below the Cover photo on your business Page, there is a box on the left side that says Status, Photo/Video, and Event, Milestone.** This is called the Composer. From this box, share or post the following:

   • **Status.** This is text about your business, its daily happenings, specials, new products, and so on. The box automatically defaults to Status and you can type in the text box where it says "Write something..."

   • **Photo/Video.** This is where you can add photos or videos that relate to your business or events that will appear on your Timeline.

   • **Event, Milestone.** By clicking on this link you can add an event for your business. You can also add milestones that your business reaches here, such as anniversaries and opening of additional locations.

2. **Once you finish adding the information you want to post on your Timeline in the appropriate box, you can choose if you want to share this with everyone by keeping it public or define exactly who you want your audience to be by targeting a location/language.**

3. **Click Share to add your post to your Timeline.**

You now have content added to your business Page Timeline for all your fans to see when they visit your Page. Again, this is a great way to share information about your business and encourage your fans to interact with your Page, as any content you share will appear in their News Feeds.

Cover photo

The cover photo is the large photo that appears at the top of your business Page. The cover photo makes a strong statement to users when they land on your Page, so you want to ensure it's something that captures the essence of your brand, product, or service (see Figure 2.8). This can be a single photo, a collage of photos, or a photo that incorporates your business logo, tagline, or other information. Whatever the image is, for the best quality it should be 851 pixels wide and 315 pixels tall and less than 100KB. If it is not these dimensions, it will be stretched to fit these dimensions, which may severely alter its appearance. Also, your cover photo may not contain the following:

- Price or purchase information (such as 50 percent off)

- Contact information that is intended for your About section, such as web address, e-mail, or mailing address

- References to use interface elements, such as *like* or *share* or any other Facebook site features

- Calls to action, such as "Get it now" or "Tell your friends"

2.8 Starbucks uses a fun photo collage as its cover photo.

Views and apps

The views and apps boxes that appear under your Cover photo represent different areas of information about your business. In addition to the standard views such as the Photos, Likes, and Events, Facebook also lets you create other Pages or add other applications such as Restaurant Reservation or Product Catalogs (see Figure 2.9).

2.9 Views and apps appear under the cover photo on your business Page and give you and your visitors quick access to the main features and applications you've added to your Page. The applications you see are specific to each individual Page and depend on what applications you've added to your Page.

While adding applications is a more advanced step and outside the bounds of this book, there are certain applications, such as the Welcome Page, that are a nice addition and easy to add (see Figure 2.10).

To add a Welcome Page from one of the applications within Facebook, follow these simple steps:

1. **From your personal Facebook Page, type** Welcome Page app **in the search box.** A list of applications appears with the most popular at the top. You can click See more results to expand the selection that the query returns.

2. **Choose the application that you want to use and click Go to App on the right.**

2.10 A Welcome Page is a nice addition to your business Page and a way to convey additional information to your visitors.

3. **Review the information on the Page and, if you have multiple Pages, choose which Page you want the app applied to.** Once you've reviewed it, click Add to My Page.

4. **The Welcome Page now appears on the business Page and can be accessed and configured by clicking Welcome in the box below your Cover photo.** With many of the applications, you now can configure and edit this Welcome Page with any specific options available.

You can follow these same steps to add other Page links or applications to your business Page. Just search for the specific application that you want to add. Be aware that while some applications are very simple to add to your Page, many others require a more advanced level of knowledge and possibly development skill.

Applying Page settings and adding admins

Once basic information and content are added to your Page, you are going to want to review your settings and manage your permissions. To review your current settings, follow these steps:

1. **Open the Admin Panel and Click Update Info from the drop-down list at the top of your Page.**

2. **In the left-hand column, click Your Settings.**

3. **You have the option on this Page to change your Posting Preference and Email Notifications.** Choose the appropriate settings.

4. **Click Save Changes to save the settings.**

Next, review the permission settings for your Page. Follow these steps:

1. **Click Manage Permissions in the left-hand column.** Here you can see your specific settings, including Country Restrictions, Age Restrictions, Posting Ability, Moderation Blocklist, Profanity Blocklist, and Delete Page (see Figure 2.11).

2. **Go through each setting and adjust to fit the needs of your Page and business.** For example, if you don't want your fans to be able to post comments to your Timeline or comment on existing posts, deselect the Everyone can post check box in the Posting Ability section.

3. **After reviewing all the settings and ensuring they are set to fit your needs, click Save Changes on the bottom of the Page.**

NOTE You can go back at any time to adjust your Page settings or permissions, should you choose.

Like any other aspect of your business marketing plan, managing your Facebook business Page takes time. As your social media engagement grows, you might find that you don't have the time to manage the Facebook Page. That's okay. The beauty of a Facebook Page is that you can ask others to moderate and manage the Page for you.

2.11 Manage your permissions to ensure that you are allowing only what and who you want on your Page.

There are five different admin roles that you can choose from, each with different capabilities. Figure 2.12 outlines each role and what it can do.

	Manager	Content Creator	Moderator	Advertiser	Insights Analyst
Manage Admin Roles	✓				
Edit the Page and Add Apps	✓	✓			
Create Posts as the Page	✓	✓			
Respond to and Delete Comments	✓	✓	✓		
Send Messages as the Page	✓	✓	✓		
Create Ads	✓	✓	✓	✓	
View Insights	✓	✓	✓	✓	✓

Permalink · Share

2.12 An overview of the five different administrative roles and their abilities.

Admins can be added and removed in the Manage Admins section of the Edit Page View as follows:

1. **Open the Admin Panel and click Edit Page.**

2. **Click Admin Roles in the left-hand column.**

3. **Type a friend's name or e-mail address in the text box to invite someone to be an admin your Page.** Below the e-mail box, choose the admin role you want this person to take on. You need to confirm your password after each entry. When you send an invite to friends, a Page Admin notification is sent to them. Once they accept the invitation, they are noted as admins on the Page.

4. **If you have additional admins to add, click Add Another Admin to access an additional entry box and repeat the previous step.**

5. **Click Save on the bottom of the Page.**

Publishing your Page

After you design your Pages, add the content you want your visitors to see, and adjust all your necessary settings, you are ready to announce to the world that your Page is up and ready for viewing! It is now time to let all your friends know that your Page is ready by sending them an invite, which you can do from your personal Facebook account using these steps:

1. **If you are on your business Page, go to your personal account by clicking the gear icon next to the Home button in the Facebook toolbar at the top of the Page and choosing your personal Page.**

2. **Click Home on the top of the Page to go to your personal home Page.**

3. **In the left-hand column you will see a listing for Pages and your Pages should appear underneath this.** Click on the Page you want to share with friends. This opens up a view of your business Page (see Figure 2.13).

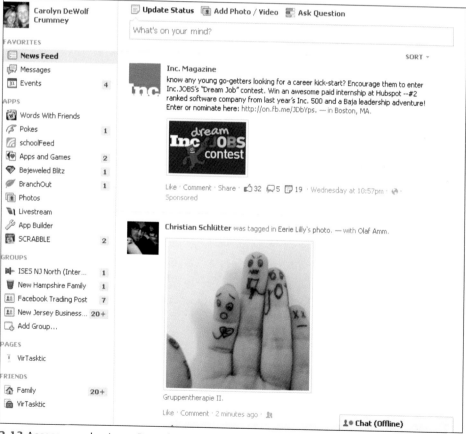

2.13 Access your business Page through your personal account in order to access your Friends list to send invitations to follow your Page.

4. **On the right side of the Admin Panel, click Build Audience, and then click Invite Friends.** Click See All to display all your Facebook friends (see Figure 2.14).

5. **Click on all the friends that you want to invite to view your Page and then click Submit.** An invitation is sent to your friends.

For more about the basics of creating a Facebook business Page, tools available, and ideas for marketing, use the Facebook Help Center.

You now have a basic Facebook business Page and can start to promote your products and services to the 1 billion users of Facebook! As you begin to see the impact that having a Facebook Page can have on your business and the reach it has to current and potential customers, you may want to consider taking your Page to the next step in design and functionality. You can do this by using a Page design tool, which is covered in the next section.

2.14 Select each friend that you want to send an announcement to view your Page.

Choosing a Page Design Tool

With the recent changes that opened up Facebook's support for content, there are numerous online services that help you design a Page and publish it to your business Page. At the time of this writing, well over a dozen capable tools are available, all with different options and capabilities. Thankfully, many of them are free for businesses just starting out and using any of them is easier than attempting to use an HTML editor and publish it manually.

While each tool has its own strengths and weaknesses, they all generally operate the same way. The following is a sample list with some recommendations based on their simplicity, pricing, and popularity.

- **Pagemodo: www.pagemodo.com (recommended).** This design tool lets you create a custom business Page in minutes. The cost varies from free to about $30 per month, depending on how many Pages you want to design. You do not need design, graphic, or coding skills to use this tool.

- **ShortStack: www.shortstack.com (recommended).** This is another design tool that allows you to create dynamic Facebook Pages in minutes. The cost of this program varies from free to $300 per month, depending on how many bells and whistles you want, all of which are clearly defined on its website. Unlike some of the other design programs, ShortStack uses widgets instead of applications, which enables you to place more than one on a Page. This allows you further customization options when designing your Page.

- **Tabfusion: www.tabfusion.com.** With Tabfusion, you can create fun and useful apps to add to your Facebook Page. These apps can either be linked to popular websites such as Twitter and YouTube or offer independent functionality. Tabfusion offers annual per application pricing plans as well as annual site-wide pricing.

- **FaceItPages: www.faceitpages.com.** With only 20 applications that you can add to your Facebook Page, FaceItPages is slightly more limited than some of the other design tools. Pricing plans vary from free to $29 per month, depending on how many active Pages you want.

- **Social Candy: www.social-candy.com/pages.** With plans ranging from $20 to $29 per month, Social Candy offers predesigned templates and applications to help you create a customized Facebook Page. (Pricing is reduced if you purchase a full-year plan.)

- **Wildfire: www.wildfireapp.com.** Wildfire is another design tool that seems to focus highly on promotion building as well as creating customized Pages. Pricing is only available by requesting a demo from its team.

You should note that some of the free design services only allow you to add a single Page (usually Welcome Page) and that many Page designer tools assume the existence of certain Pages and cannot create them for you. Therefore, you should be very thorough when choosing a Page design tool to ensure it will fit your needs and accomplish everything you are looking for.

Other options

Apart from the services focused specifically on Facebook Page design in the preceding list, other tools are available that may work with the website content you already have. WordPress (http://wordpress.org) offers a plug-in that gives you Facebook-oriented templates and also lets you publish changes directly. The website designer Wix (www.wix.com) also offers similar capabilities with a vast collection of jazzy templates.

Selecting a design

There are many options for your Page design in each of the applications listed previously. You can select from a library of predefined Page templates and backgrounds, or you can create your own from images you provide. Just as when you are designing your business website, you want to make sure that the design you choose reflects the style and character of your business.

Adding promotions

Some designers provide an optional advanced step that enables you to run Check-in Deals, contests, sweepstakes, and other marketing events within your Page. While these items can be very powerful social marketing mechanisms, it's a good idea to start with a simple Page first and then advance to this type of application once you get your feet wet. I talk more about promotions and how to add them in Chapter 3.

Establishing a Facebook connection

Any Page design tool that you choose requires you to use your Facebook login to retrieve the specifics of your business Page and to be able to publish later. There is no reason to fear providing this information because the login info transmitted using feature that directly connects Facebook to the Page design tool and is not maintained anywhere other than by Facebook.

Best Practices in Design and Content

Beyond the mechanics of which tool to use and the steps to follow, there are some key considerations in the design and maintenance of your Facebook business Page. These principles are part of what make the difference between a business Page that is bland and one that is truly compelling.

Take the easy path: Use a Page design tool

The easiest way to create a spectacular Page is to use one of the Page design tools referenced earlier. It's simple, inexpensive (if not free), and lets you focus your time on more important endeavors, like marketing ideas. Page design tools are equipped with all the tools you need to create an interactive Page, and most offer an array of applications that you may want to consider to add "Wow" to your Page.

Use simple and expressive visuals

With the limited space you have, utilize simple, evocative images that communicate a single clear message. While theoretically possible, simply reproducing a website's home page on your business Page is not a good practice. The nature and psychology of interaction on Facebook is different than that of visitors accessing a website. Stick with simple, but make it unique and interesting!

Get creative with profile image and photos

Because Facebook is a visual medium, the more creative and visually stimulating you make your profile photo and cover photo, the more intrigued your visitors will be to stay on your Page and learn more about your business.

Profile photo

Use an image that scales well from 180 × 180 to 32 × 32 pixels. Anything larger is scaled. At a minimum, you should choose an image that displays your entire logo and business name without truncation.

Cover photo

Although the intent of the cover photo is to show an overall image related to your business, some creative business Pages repurpose them as part of the overall Page design (see Figure 2.15).

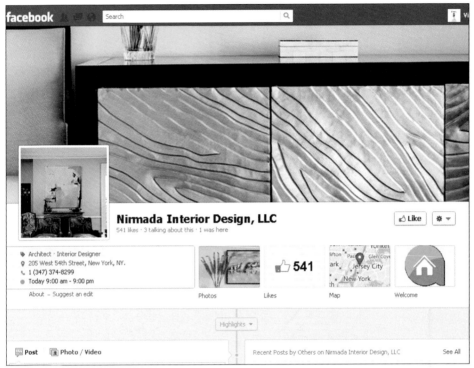

2.15 Your cover photo can become a major part of your overall Page design and aesthetic.

Another unique way to use your cover photo is to display individual products that you sell or services you provide. This gives visitors a strong first impression of your business and what it is you do (see Figure 2.16).

Inject your personality

As you've likely heard by now, social media and marketing are first and foremost about presenting an authentic persona to your community. This practice doesn't mean eroding your business's professionalism, but it simply acknowledges and is empowered by the notion that there are humans behind it all.

So in the design of your business Page, your posts, or elsewhere in your interaction, try to find ways to cut through the formality. While it's hard to provide a formula for being authentic, here are a few tips:

- Steer clear of stock images and use real pictures of your business.

- Present your work where possible. Whether it's the favorite dessert at your restaurant or an exceptional renovation project, you always want to give your visitors a visual of your business and its product or services.

- Use conversational language, not business jargon, and eliminate superfluous, unwieldy language.

2.16 The cover photo can become an additional selling tool to display your products to visitors who come to your Page.

Follow Facebook guidelines

Generally, Facebook doesn't impose overly broad restrictions on content on your business Page, but promotional activities that involve gaming or contests require you to navigate carefully within the company's terms and conditions.

- Contests, sweepstakes, giveaways, or any marketing involving a winner or a prize is required to be administered via a registered third-party app on a separate page.

- You can give away a prize or incentive for fans who like your Page, but again, through a separate page.

- Any promotional campaign Pages need to clearly link to the Facebook terms and conditions content from the main Page.

To see all the guidelines for running a contest or promotion, go to www.facebook.com/promotions_guidelines.php.

Engage, don't educate

Your Page is not the place to provide a dissertation on your business's core values or all the services you offer. Ditch the bio, or anything with multiple lines of text. Think of it as a cocktail party conversation starter and start with something simple and engaging — an expressive picture, a provocative statement, or a question or poll to your followers.

You have a very limited amount of time to portray your business to a visitor that comes to your Page. Make an impact when your Page opens! Provide pictures and content that will intrigue them and encourage them to stay and search through your content.

Refresh often

Just as with a blog, refresh the elements of your Page often to maintain interest and provide reassurance that your business presence is well tended. You can create excitement within your fan base if you are constantly creating new content on your Page. Here are ideas on how to keep your Page fresh:

- **Rotate among different variations of your profile image.** You can have seasonal versions or overlay different promotional messages on the same image.

- **Post photos wisely.** Keep the photos flowing, but stay true to a theme such as happy-customer photos, prepared entrees, or even abstract imagery.

- **Contests, coupons, and other promotional content should have a limited lifespan.** Try to rotate among different Welcome Pages or coupon offers, even if the changes are minor tweaks to messaging or imagery.

Case Study: It's a Perfect Day

Some businesses have perfected the task of putting all the right elements needed for success on their Facebook business Page. One such company is It's a Perfect Day. The following is a descriptive of who the company is, what its founder did that was right, and what he was able to achieve with his Facebook business Page.

It's a Perfect Day is a designer of custom T-shirts and apparel that convey the simple notion that every day is perfect for something (see Figure 2.17).

This is a classic story of creativity and entrepreneurism that is emblematic of small-businesses everywhere. The business was started as a creative outlet for its founder, Satya Kommini, a Microsoft product manager, who was seeking a new path inspired by the novel *Eat, Pray, Love*. Utilizing his own untapped artistic talent and a hardworking team led by his supportive wife, It's a Perfect Day launched in July 2011, selling 17 designs of apparel all based on a singular notion of gratitude and optimism. Using no advertising other than his Facebook Page and word-of-mouth marketing of his story, Kommini was able to reach 535 likes in less than three weeks.

So how did Kommini and his team do it? They recognized the key attributes of a successful Facebook Page, like those outlined earlier in this chapter. They used simple and expressive images on their Welcome Page that intrigued visitors but didn't overwhelm them. They injected personality and whimsy with eye-catching photos. They offered a promotion to those landing on the Page, which engaged the visitor immediately. Their Page is simple yet relays all the pertinent information you need to understand their product and make purchases, should you choose. The Page is engaging, not educating. All in all, they designed a Page that serves the exact needs of a Facebook business Page.

2.17 It's a Perfect Day has created a perfect Welcome Page, including unique photos, strong content, and an opportunity for the visitor to engage.

chapter 3

Timeline Info Photos Notes

Drawing More People to Your Page

You can drive additional people to your business Page by using contests, polls, and questions. By incorporating these items into your Page, you add a much-desired variety to your postings. Instead of arriving at a Timeline full of status updates, customers first see a few interactive pieces that directly ask them to participate. These Facebook apps also create ways to encourage customers to communicate with you when they may not know exactly what to share.

The most powerful way a company can build its community on Facebook is through audience engagement. This chapter covers how to use Facebook apps to bring interactivity to your business Page.

Creating Contests, Polls, and Questions

Your Facebook business Page will not be a successful part of your marketing plan if you can't get people to visit your Page. Encourage people to visit your Page and interact with your business by using contests, polls, and questions.

Contests

People love contests and sweepstakes. The opportunity to beat the odds and win a contest, even with a one-in-a-million chance, is alluring. Facebook has features for incorporating and managing a contest on your Page (see Figure 3.1). These contests are run by third-party vendors, not Facebook.

3.1 Contests are a great addition to your Facebook business Page or group.

Quote, Unquote: Facebook and Contests

"Facebook has been the most effective with respect to contests. Research shows that, while small-business owners may not engage actively with their vendors on Facebook, they are very receptive to deals and contests. One of the reasons for effectiveness in this area is the tools. Facebook requires a third-party tool be used to run contests on its platform. As a result, the ecosystem of available tools is much more mature compared to the other social networks."

— Greg Tirico, senior social media manager for Sage, a global business software and services company.

This chapter covers the basics of creating a contest on Facebook. Contests can attract visitors to a Facebook fan Page or serve as a supplement for a Check-in campaign. A *Check-in campaign* is a way to drive repeat traffic to a local store — the more people Check-in via Facebook, the more points they receive for a chance to win something. Many businesses have seen success with contests.

All contests promoted on Facebook *must* use a Facebook-approved app. There are absolutely no exceptions. Facebook monitors businesses to ensure that promotions fall within its guidelines, and it can penalize a company by removing content and disabling a Facebook Page. Read Facebook promotion guidelines here: www.facebook.com/ promotions_guidelines.php.

Fortunately, a number of contest applications are available, each providing services perfect for creating contests, sweepstakes, coupons, polls, or other promotions. These apps provide various data collection methods for the contest, such as entry forms within the app link or an e-mail form. The most common applications currently available are the following:

- Wildfire (www.wildfireapp.com)
- North Social (http://northsocial.com)
- Woobox (http://woobox.com)
- Votigo (www.votigo.com)
- Strutta (www.strutta.com)
- Offerpop (http://offerpop.com)

You can search for all these applications on Facebook or on websites such as Appbistro (http://appbistro.com) or All Facebook (http://allfacebook.com). You can also use sources such as Mashable to research contest success stories from various businesses to decide what type of contest or promotion might be most effective for your business.

Contests, like other promoted content online, take time to promote. Try to promote a contest or sweepstakes at least a few weeks before its starting date and then run the contest or sweepstakes for at least two to three weeks, if possible. You need time for the news about the contest to spread and for people to participate.

Facebook ads can be used to market your contest (as long as the content adheres to guidelines). The ad-creation process is, of course, the same as for standard Facebook ads. You have to ensure the ads link to your registration page or a landing page that explains the contest or sweepstakes. Make sure that you have a few images for your ads, especially if the promotion is lengthy. Different images may prevent the ad from appearing old, while the new images can help generate interest, if not a lot of clicks.

Also consider focusing ads on particular demographics or regions. You can use the Ads Manager (discussed in depth in Chapter 4) to determine how well the ads are doing. These ads can augment your other marketing efforts to build your contest audience. You can access your Ads Manager and read more about Facebook Ad Guidelines here: http://ads.ak.facebook.com/ads/FacebookAds/TheNewAdsManager_May2011v2.pdf.

You can also create and send video messages about your contests. Share these with your Page followers and ask partners to mention your sweepstakes in their posts or podcasts.

Polls

Facebook polls are another way to engage with your customers, gain insight from your Facebook audience, and start conversations. Polls, of course, seek insights from people regarding topics. I suggest you create short questions with multiple-choice answers. The polls you create display your care for customer opinions and enable you to discover ways to improve communication with your followers. This can lead to new ideas for your Page and refreshing the engagement (see Figure 3.2).

Question of the Day: If you are a small business owner, how many hours   ✕
do you work per week? - Andrea

☐ **40-60**   ...

☐ **60-80**   ...

☐ **20-40**   ...

☐ **All of them**   ...

＋ Add an answer...

5 More ▾

Asked By   233 Votes · 3 Followers

Social Media Examiner
about 2 months ago · 🌐 · Share · Report   🚩 **Ask Friends**   **+1 Follow**

Posts   Friends · Others (5)

3.2 Creating a poll generates additional interaction from your members and offers valuable insight to your business. Polls can be created daily or at any frequency level you choose; just keep in mind they are designed to create interaction between your company and your followers.

The steps to creating a traditional poll, one in which you specify all the options up front and people may not vote for more than one option, are quite simple:

1. **Click the Event, Milestone link beneath the cover photo section of your home Page and then click Question (see Figure 3.3).**

2. **Type your question in the Ask Something box.**

3. **Click Add Poll Options to enter the answers you want to have as options.**

Let us help you with the tasks that are taking too much time out of your day...

So you can spend your precious time on the things that make you more successful ...professionally and personally!

VirTasktic
28 likes

Consulting/Business Services
We are the FanTASKtic Virtual Assistants!

Photos   Likes   Events   Livestream

About

Highlights ▼

📝 Status   📷 Photo / Video   📅 Event, Milestone +

📅 Event
📖 Milestone
📊 Question

3.3 The first step to adding a poll to your business Page is to click Event, Milestone and then click Question.

4. **Deselect the Allow anyone to add options check box if you want your poll to only contain the responses you supplied.** If you want to create a poll where people can add options, ensure that the Allow anyone to add options check box is selected (see Figure 3.4).

5. **Click the settings gear box to choose additional targeting options, which include language and country.**

6. **Click Post.** Your question is posted to your Timeline and sent to your users (or only those who meet your targeted criteria).

```
🖹 Status      📷 Photo / Video      31 Event, Milestone +

What is your favorite social media platform?


   Facebook

   Twitter

   LinkedIn

 + Pinterest

 + Add an option...

 ☐ Allow anyone to add options          🌐 Public  ▼      Post
```

3.4 Type your question and a selection of answers that your followers can choose from to answer. Deselect the Allow anyone to add options check box to ensure that only your answers appear as choices.

Here are some tips to make polls successful:

- Keep poll subjects short.

- Make questions as direct as possible.

- Only ask one question — avoid compound questions.

- Post the results as soon as possible. For a weekly poll, give the results weekly; for a daily poll, give the results daily.

There are a number of Facebook tools you can use to encourage participation. For example, send a video message to some of your followers. The message can alert them to the poll or be a reminder to participate. Be careful you don't go overboard in reaching out to followers. Contact them too much and you can start spamming them, but contact them too little and they'll forget you. Be balanced.

Once your poll is complete, be sure to share some behind-the-scenes perspective with the results. Create a blog post that elaborates on the results and draws conclusions. Share the information on your Facebook Page, either through your notes or a post on your Page's Timeline. If you have feedback, you can share the comments anonymously.

Questions

Another way to further engage your fans is to set up an environment for them to ask questions that are shared publicly. Facebook lets users ask a question and get quick answers from their friends and other people on Facebook. A poll has predefined options for the potential answers, and a question is where the respondents provide their own answers. Questions are designed so that anyone on Facebook can help you find the answer, so when you ask a question it is shared in your friends' News Feeds. If your friends answer or follow that question, it is shared with their friends, and so on.

You can ask any type of question you want, but remember that questions are designed for fast, short-form responses. For example, you can use questions to get recommendations from your customers (What are your favorite business apps that you use while traveling?), learn more about the people within the group (What drew you to this line of business?), or start discussion about current events (How can I help reduce the unemployment levels in our industry?).

Anyone on Facebook may answer a question you ask, but answers are always filtered to show you only the responses from your followers. To access the responses from anyone else, click Others within the Posts section of the question.

Questions can yield some excellent results for your business. It did for Dell, according to my friend Laura Thomas, corporate reputation manager for Dell's global commercial channel vice president/general manager. She told me in an interview that "It's a very easy way to get a quick response to serious questions that can provide feedback for business decisions, or for fun questions that just help build a sense of camaraderie with Page fans."

Additional Ways to Drive More Facebook Visits

There are a number of ways to make your presence on Facebook an attractive draw for customers and clients alike. You can create a poll, create sweepstakes or contests, share blog posts that are related to your Page, announce Check-in campaigns, and run Facebook ads. But do you think that's all? Of course not! Your business can apply some advanced methodologies to drive more traffic to your Facebook Page. Although it may seem like a hassle, keep in mind that your business can already drive this traffic naturally in many ways, so the effort is not necessarily an extra task. My goal is to show you how you can make the most of the Facebook audience.

Include a link to Facebook in your business material

Make sure your business materials reflect that you have a Facebook presence. This may sound like a simple act, but you would be surprised how many small businesses over-look this opportunity to provide a coherent message. You should make incorporating Facebook (and truthfully, all your social media presences) a habit so that it's second nature to have a card or pamphlet that shows where and how people can join your busi-ness on Facebook.

You can have a sticker in your store window that reminds customers to go to your Facebook Page. Brochures for your services can display the fan Page with the ubiquitous Facebook symbol next to it, the address of your Page, and a note to "Join Us." You can do the same for the ending and beginning of video you create. The key is providing some reminder of your media property and asking people to join you there (see Figure 3.5).

3.5 This business owner has created a business card that ensures that you can find her on every social media site that she belongs to.

Online small-business service directories like Manta allow user profiles to include a link to a Facebook business Page. Another service, an app called WiseStamp, includes Facebook comments within the closing of an e-mail. This can be a draw for followers used to seeing a simple Facebook fan Page name at the end of their e-mail.

Your badges or links should send potential customers to the portion of your business Page where they can engage and listen most naturally. Doing so tells your customers they can ask questions to learn more about your services and how to ultimately reach you when they are ready to do business.

Make your Page name simple

When you first set up your business Page, you are given a standard fan Page URL, which is a series of random numbers that are not very easily remembered. The first thing to do is to create a username for your Page. Usernames allow you to easily promote your presence on Facebook and can be used in your marketing communications, company website, and business cards. Creating a username gives your Page a specific name that becomes the URL for your business Page. Use the name of your business as the username, if it is available. For example, if your business name is Acme Printing, then make your username AcmePrinting, and the corresponding URL would be https://www.facebook.com/AcmePrinting. You can follow these steps to change your Page username:

1. **On the upper-right corner of your business Page, click Admin Panel.**

2. **At the top of the Page, click Edit Page.**

3. **From the list of links on the left side, choose Resources (see Figure 3.6).**

3.6 Changing your Page username is simple! Click Edit Page under the Admin Tools, and then click Resources in the left-hand column and choose Select a username from the available options on the Page.

4. **Choose Select a username from the list of available resources.** If you are currently using Facebook as your business Page, you will be asked to continue under your personal account.

5. **Choose which Page you want to create a username for from the drop-down list.** If you have only one Page, the name of that Page shows by default (see Figure 3.7).

6. **Choose a username for your Page by typing the name of your business in the box and then click Check Availability.**

7. **If the name is available, confirm that you want to make the change by clicking Confirm.** Once you confirm, your new URL that you can use in your marketing materials is displayed.

facebook | Search   🔍 |

Each Page can have a username
Easily direct someone to your Page by setting a username for it. You will not be able to edit or transfer this username once you set it.

Page Name: VirTasktic ▾   Enter desired username

Check Availability

3.7 Type in the name you want to assign as your username and check its availability. If it's available, click Confirm and your username is changed.

All names are given on a first-come, first-serve basis, so if your business uses a widely used word in its name, you may find that it is unavailable. If that happens, get creative when choosing your name but remember not to defer too far from your business name, as it may make it difficult for people to find you.

You should also remember that your Page is searchable through search engines outside of Facebook. This means that you may want to incorporate a keyword in the title to help your business be discovered.

NOTE You may want to control how exposed a Page is to search, particularly at the launch stage when you are still making adjustments and edits. To hide your Page from search engines, go to the privacy settings and deselect the Public Search check box.

Once content is already online and indexed by search engines it's hard to take it down. To remove online content, try these two steps:

- **Delete the original post.** This is probably the easiest option of the two given here. When you do this, the content may still show up in search engines, but the link to that content is invalid.

- **Contact the specific search engine's support team.** If you want the entire search result to go away, you need to contact the search engine to remove it. Each search engine will have a different process to contact them — e-mail, phone, an online form, or other means.

Tag people

Another great way to attract more people to your Page is by tagging photos that you post on your Page. Tagging is identifying a person in a photo as one of your Facebook friends. Tagging photos on your business Page tells your fans that they are noticed and appreciated and gives others the chance to see firsthand how you interact with your customers and business partners.

Upload photos from seminars, panel discussions, and trade shows you attend and tag as many people that you recognize in the photo as possible. Once you tag people in a photo, they receive a notification on their own Page that they have been tagged in your photo. This invariably leads them, and any of their friends who see the post on their Page, to your Page. Tagging a photo is quite simple:

1. **After you upload your photo to Facebook, click Tag Photo on the lower-right of the picture.**

2. **Click on the image of the person you want to tag in the photo and a small box appears on the photo.**

3. **Type the name of the person in the photo.** If the person is a fan or friend of yours, his or her name appears in the list to choose. If the person is not a fan or friend, as you type in the name, a list of potential names appears. These names belong to groups or public figures. Make sure you do not improperly tag the photo with the wrong name (see Figure 3.8).

Many businesses take advantage of mobile phone cameras to make photo sharing and tagging really effective. You can take pictures of customers in your retail shop during an event or sale and then instantly post them to your Page and tag the customers while they are still in your shop. Another great idea is to ask your patrons to take photos of themselves wearing your business T-shirt, button, or other promotional item, and then upload them to their Page and tag your business. In both instances, you are exposing your business to an endless number of people on Facebook.

3.8 Tagging people in photos is a great way to establish additional interaction on your Page.

Participate in forums

Participating in forums is a great way to promote your business and, through good forum discussion, drive fans to your Facebook Page. You may be working in an industry where participating in the industry forum is essential for being visible. That forum can be on a number of platforms, from Ning to LinkedIn. When you do participate, see how you can enhance the forum discussions. Be careful not to overpromote, however, and follow community guidelines about bold promotional efforts. People usually are grateful for helpful and meaningful participation, so learn how to be a good neighbor. Your signature in each forum post can provide a link to your Facebook Page.

Encourage fans

Do not be too controlling of who promotes your product. Discouraging fans that suddenly create a Page about your business may do more harm than good. A great example of cooperation is cited in the 2010 *Harvard Business Review* article "Empowered" by Josh Bernoff and Ted Schadler. Coca-Cola discovered an unauthorized Facebook fan Page about its soda by two raving Coca-Cola fans who wanted to share their love for Coke with others. Their site became one of the most popular fan Pages on Facebook.

Instead of using legal action to take the fan site down, Coke partnered with its fans. The fans were given a rare tour of Coca-Cola headquarters and Coke allowed its fans to direct their customer engagement. This did not take anything away from Coke, and it really enhanced the company's standing online.

The point is that it's good to listen and be aware of who your fans are and what they are saying, and know when it may be better to use a good comment or fan Page to your advantage.

Make it easy for folks to share

The Coke story is not just an example of control but of simplicity. Imagine the resources and time Coke would have had to invest to replace Song and Jedrzejweski's Page with its own. It was much easier to keep the ball rolling with the content they had already created and the following they had generated. Though your business is most likely on a smaller scale (and probably involves much less soda), you should always keep such simplicity in mind when you seek interaction from your followers.

If you request content from your followers, make it an easy act. The request can range from a simple photo post to a simple thought or comment in a Timeline post. Remember that their time is as precious as yours. The easier you make it to fulfill the request for content, the easier it is to generate engagement and maintain the vitality of your Page.

Using Groups

Groups provide a way to engage a dedicated audience. Groups are more private than Pages, but they provide a means to share information and receive feedback with a highly engaging set of people.

How are Pages different from groups?

Groups are more private than Pages, but their privacy creates a community within Facebook. This may be convenient for businesses that need to communicate with clients closely and continuously to provide faster service and retain customers in a competitive field. Pages, on the other hand, are public and can be accessed by anyone. Interaction on the Page is typically open to anyone who visits, unless it is specified that you like the Page before you can add comments and interactions, and most of the interaction is generated by you in an effort to inform visitors about your business.

Pages enable real organizations, businesses, celebrities, and brands to communicate broadly with people who like them. Pages may only be created and managed by official representatives.

Groups provide a closed space for small groups of people to communicate about shared interests. Groups can be created by anyone.

Other differences include the following:

Pages

- **Privacy.** Page information and posts are public and generally available to everyone on Facebook.

- **Audience.** Anyone can like a Page to become connected with it and get News Feed updates. There is no limit to how many people can like a Page.

- **Communication.** Page administrators can share posts under the Page's name. Page posts appear in the News Feed of people who like the Page. Page admins can also create customized app links for their Pages and check Page Insights to track the Page's growth and activity.

Groups

- **Privacy.** In addition to an open setting, more privacy settings are available for groups. In secret and closed groups, posts are only visible to group members.

- **Audience.** Group members must be approved or added by other members. When a group reaches a certain size, some features are limited. The most useful groups tend to be the ones you create with small groups of people you know.

- **Communication.** In groups, members receive notifications by default when any member posts in the group. Group members can participate in chats, upload photos to shared albums, collaborate on group docs, and invite all members to group events.

How do I set up a group?

Creating a group is as simple as creating a Page. Follow these simple steps to get started:

1. **On the left side of your personal home Page, under the Groups section, click Add Group.** (If you have existing groups, you may need to click More before you see this link.) If you don't have a Groups section, go to www.facebook.com/groups to add a group.

2. **Click Create a New Group if accessing from your home Page (see Figure 3.9) or click Create Group if accessing from the web address (see Figure 3.10).**

3. **Choose a name for your group and type it in the Group Name box.**

4. **Add members to your group.** Type names in the box and then choose them from the drop-down list of names that appear matching your search.

Add a group name, select your members, and set the group privacy

Click Add Group to open the group Page

3.9 This image shows the path of creating a group from your home Page.

3.10 This image shows the path of creating a group through the web link.

5. **Select the appropriate privacy setting for your group.** There are three levels of privacy:

   - **Open.** Everyone on Facebook can view the group and join. The group appears in search results and all content (photos, videos, and discussions) is visible to anyone viewing the group.

   - **Closed.** Everyone on Facebook can see the name and members of a group, but only group members can view content in the group.

   - **Secret.** These groups cannot be found in searches, and nonmembers can't see anything about the group, including its name and membership list. The name of the group is not displayed on members' profiles.

6. **Create the Group by clicking Create at the bottom of the pop-up box.**

If you are unsure of the privacy setting you should select, don't fear. If your group has 250 members or less, your admins can adjust the privacy settings of the group after it's been created by clicking the settings icon and selecting Edit Group at the upper-right corner of the group Page. All members of the group will receive a notification that the settings have changed.

Once the group is created, you are taken to the group's Page. You can set the group settings by clicking the settings icon at the top of the Page and selecting Edit Group (see Figure 3.11). Here you can add a group description, set a group e-mail address, add a group picture, and manage members (see Figure 3.12).

3.11 To edit the group, click on the settings gear icon and then choose Edit Group.

New Hampshire Family	About	Events	Photos	Files

Group Name: New Hampshire Family

Privacy:
○ **Open**
Anyone can see the group, who's in it, and what members post.

○ **Closed**
Anyone can see the group and who's in it. Only members see posts.

◉ **Secret**
Only members see the group, who's in it, and what members post.

Membership Approval:
◉ Any member can add or approve members.
○ Any member can add members, but an admin must approve them.

Email Address: Set Up Group Email

Description:

Potential members see the description if privacy is set to open or closed.

Posting Permissions:
◉ Only members can post in this group.
○ Only administrators can post to the group.

Save

3.12 Once in the group editing field, you can add a group description, set the group e-mail address, add a group picture, and manage members.

Once a group is created, set a group e-mail address to help your group stay in touch. Follow these steps:

1. **On the top-right of the group Page, click the settings gear icon and then click Edit Group.**

2. **Click Set Up Group Email.**

3. **Type an e-mail address for your group.** No special characters can be used — the e-mail address can only include letters, numbers, and periods.

4. **Click Create Email.** If the e-mail address you picked is available, it becomes your group e-mail. If it's taken, you need to choose a different e-mail. Once your group e-mail address has been set, it cannot be changed.

5. **Click Save.**

Only members of the group are able to use this e-mail address. When a member sends an e-mail to this address, the message is posted in the group and other members are notified. If a group member responds to an e-mail, the response appears as a comment on the group post.

If you want to have a social media team or another group member manage your group, your current admin must add more admins to the group so they have access and control of the group. Keep in mind that admins can remove members or admins, add new admins, and edit the group description and settings. You should only add members as admins if you already know and trust them.

To include additional admins, follow these steps:

1. **On the group Page, click on the link *X* members (where *X* is the number of members in the group) under the group name.**

2. **Find a member by typing a name in the search box.**

3. **Click Make Admin next to the name of the member you want to add as admin.**

The group admin can set who can approve requests to join the group. If you only want admins to be able to approve the request, follow these steps:

1. **On the top-right of the group Page, click the settings gear icon and choose Edit Group.**

2. **Select the Only admins can approve requests to join check box.**

3. **Click Save at the bottom of the Page.** Now only admins can approve members' requests to join the group. When members add friends to the group, those friends need to be approved by admins before becoming members.

How do people join my group?

People search for groups by name and interest. Once they find a group they want to join, they simply click Ask to Join Group in the upper-right corner of the group's Page. A person can also be added to a group by a friend who is already a member that submits a request for him or her to join.

Depending on the privacy setting of your group, a member may be able to join immediately or may require admin approval to join. If your group is closed, make sure that your admins are constantly reviewing and approving requests to join your Page so there are no delays. If you receive a request from a person you do not want as a member to the group, your admins can deny the request and block that specific person from joining a group.

If your group is secret, it does not appear in search results and people cannot request to join. You only gain members by sending individual invitations to people that you want to include in the group.

Just like on your business Page, you can share photos, questions, links, and other posts within your group and on your group Page. And just as with your business Page, you want to keep the content on your group Page fresh and engaging so that your members stay interested and are encouraged to interact.

How do I poll a group?

One way to encourage interaction of your group is by creating a poll, posing a question to your group members to gain opinions. This is the same as creating a poll on your business Page, but it is specific to your group and only seen by your group members. To create a poll within your group, follow the same steps as listed earlier in this chapter for your business Page.

How do I find a specific post in a group?

If you want to search for a specific post in your group, use the Search This Group box at the top right of your group Page. The search results will show the part of the post where your search words appear. Click the search results to see the original post.

How do I delete a group?

There may be a time when you feel a group has run its course or may not have the amount of engagement you expected. If you created the group, you can delete it by removing all members and then yourself. To remove members from a group, on the right side of the group select See All in the members section. Next select an X next to each member's name you wish to delete.

If you had no members, you can do nothing. Facebook automatically deletes groups that have no members after a certain amount of time. If you were not the first admin and creator of the group, you cannot delete the group unless the group creator has left it voluntarily.

Managing Backlash

So far this chapter has covered what to do to gain Facebook fans and followers and how super easy it can be with a few reminders. It can also be super easy to get into trouble with negative reactions to an announcement.

The first rule is to respond to fan posts quickly. Posts should not linger unanswered. A nonresponse sends the message that you don't care about your Page followers, which only angers them further. Moreover, a nonresponse tells other followers that you are unconcerned with customer support, which can be detrimental to your reputation.

A response that illustrates respect and understanding for customers' concerns is an indicator of your business' intention to rectify problems. So it is very important to ensure that you have someone in your business responsible for addressing posts from less-than-happy customers.

Quote, Unquote: Listening to Fans

"Social media begins with an understanding of what consumers and influencers are saying about your brand, product, or service and then builds on that through participation (yours and theirs) for the purpose of encouraging higher forms of engagement, up to and including collaboration."

— Dave Evans, author of *Social Media Marketing: The Next Generation of Business Engagement* (Wiley, 2010)

Responses can make things worse if not managed well. Just ask Honda. Honda encountered negative buzz when it introduced a new vehicle based on one of its most popular models, the Accord. The Accord Crosstour was a five-door vehicle with all-wheel drive. Honda decided to introduce the car on Facebook. The shape was different from what a traditional Accord buyer had typically seen. The body was a cross between a hatchback and an SUV. Moreover, when Honda decided to introduce the car exclusively on Facebook, the first few pictures revealed the car in a basic white color that did not flatter its shape. The reaction from Honda enthusiasts and auto fans (reported by car blog Autoblog and other automotive media outlets) was harsh. They did not like the car's appearance. Many posted statements comparing it to a noted unloved car, the Pontiac Aztek, while traditional Honda enthusiasts complained that they preferred a different body style, a wagon, over the Crosstour's hatchback/SUV hybrid approach.

Honda's response to the negative comments it received on Facebook only made matters worse. According to Autoblog, rather than acknowledging its customers' comments and opinions, Honda insisted that the vehicle should be accepted. Moreover, comments were deleted from the fan Page, including one comment that was posted by a Honda product planner.

The following sections outline some of the most important lessons on managing fan backlash.

Do not be overly insistent on your point of view

Indeed, you want to support your offering and present it in the most positive light possible, with the most accurate information. Be mindful of the replies to your efforts, but do not be condescending to those commenting. Carefully consider the right way to respond to a negative post. A good PR firm with experience in social media may be worth the expense to review the comments on your Page, but in most cases people are just looking to be heard. Be an active listener and show genuine understanding of what is being said. Be authentic.

Do not delete comments

Deleting comments is a big negative for a number of reasons. First, it shows people that you are controlling behavior and tells them that they must say the right thing to be heard. Guide your conversations in social media; don't outright edit what is not spam. Second, you never want to hijack the conversation. If there is a debate, address it with enlightening information, but never discount what the person has typed. Beyond spam, consider deleting a Timeline post that contains threats, profanity, racial slurs, and pornography. Consider creating a Posting Policy that spells out what is and isn't acceptable.

It is understandable that you would want to prevent negative information from spreading, but also remember to take criticism as an opportunity to do better at managing a situation and improving your products and services. Many small businesses have learned not to fear the feedback but instead to use it as a way to truly improve their business.

Consider judgment in using planted posts

Having support from those outside a business is not a crime. It's natural for a blog to have supporters who help with affirmative comment. But here's the rub: People with a vested interest in the product, service, or event should disclose their relationship with the topic when making comments on a blog or Facebook Page. You want authenticity in the replies as much as the post itself. You want real language and real explanations.

Not only is disclosure an ethos of social media but also the effort can create more negative buzz that spreads farther than anticipated. Moreover, in some instances, nondisclosure can hurt other aspects of a business as an underhanded act. In 2007, the FTC investigated Whole Foods CEO John Mackey when it was discovered that he had posted seemingly negative comments about then rival Wild Oats under a pseudonym. He did this for seven years! Although Mackey was cleared, the effort nearly compromised a Whole Foods acquisition of Wild Oats.

In short, be ready to disclose those who have been posting to your Facebook Page and not disclosing who they are. If you are working with an employee team, encourage members to inform others who they are and avoid harsh debates when possible.

An automobile is a difficult product to market on social media. Negative comments like those regarding the Crosstour can be hard to deflect when a product aspect is set, such as a vehicle's overall shape. But many times people want to be heard rather than feel that their comments have been diminished. Use comments to develop future refinements as well as develop new ways to respond to customers. In many cases, customers can forgive a faux paus when they see a business make an effort to respond to feedback.

Social Media Examiner offers the following thoughts to address problem posts:

- **Be patient and understanding.**

    In dealing with upset fans, you must remember that you are closer to your industry, products, and services than they are. What may seem like basic, common knowledge to you is often foreign to the end user.

    Take a step back and put yourself in your customer's shoes. This can go a long way in understanding why he or she is frustrated. It may not be your company's fault that the customer is upset.

Whether or not the fault lies on your end, a simple apology will go a long way in keeping the customer's business. Instead of trying to figure out where the blame lies, turn upset fans into loyal customers by making their experience better.

Contact the customer privately.

Sending a private message or e-mail to the customer opens up more options for you to address his or her complaints. The goal here is to extend some sort of token, letting the customer know you're sorry he or she is dissatisfied with your company and you're willing to make it right. Whether that's offering the number of the manager's direct phone line or a discount off the next purchase, moving the conversation from public to private allows you to give the customer a personal touch that signals you care.

However, offering things like direct lines and special discounts publicly can lead to other people creating problems just to get that special treatment, so it's best to keep these practices off the Timeline.

Consider asking the fan to remove the post.

Say you've discussed the issue privately, any problems have been straightened out, and the faultfinder is, once again, your happy customer.

While your Timeline is an integral part of your web presence, the customer may be unaware of how important it really is to your reputation. If he or she is satisfied with the resolution you've reached and grateful for the time you've spent making things right, there's nothing wrong with privately asking the person to remove the post. Most of the time, he or she will remove the angry Timeline post.

Respond back to the original post.

As a general rule, you, the Facebook Page admin, should not remove negative posts. Not everyone is going to have a glowing review of your product or company. Social media users know this, and if they see nothing but positive comments, they'll assume your company is deleting the bad comments.

If you don't feel comfortable asking your customer to remove the post, you do have the option of publicly responding back to that post. Express happiness in the resolution you've reached and thankfulness for her business. Even a negative post can be a good thing, as long as the last comment is positive. Your reputation among your community will soar when they see how well you take care of your customers.

Having a helpful attitude effectively nullifies any poor reflection on your business or its services.

Quote, Unquote: Facebook and Comments

"We find that people leave their least filtered comments on Facebook. Our customers have no hesitation letting us know when they love or hate our newest product! Our advice on this would be grin and bear it. It's better that your customers care enough about your product to give you feedback than to not give you any feedback at all."

— Sander Daniels, cofounder and director of business development at Thumbtack (a website connecting service providers to customers)

⚙ Let your community respond.

Letting your community respond for you is really the end result of all the earlier steps. It requires copious time, energy, and patience with your fans, and a fantastic product. After you've engaged with your fans for a period of time by answering questions and offering support, you'll notice that your fans will be more active on your Page, even to the point of assisting each other.

What's great about getting this community support is that there's a genuine credibility when fans endorse your business for you. They become your eager virtual support agents, answering questions and solving problems before you have a chance to. But this is a level you can only achieve if you've nurtured and supported your community.

Using Social Media Dashboards

Sharing information about your business on multiple social media sites can be very time consuming. Going from Twitter to Facebook to StumbleUpon to the company blog can be dizzying enough to wear out any small-business social media manager. Moreover, managing multiple platforms in a standard browser can lead to errors, such as posting on one account but forgetting to post to another. You may overlook your supporters who spend most of their time following your blog, reading your Facebook statuses, or reading your tweets.

To save time and effort, you, your social media manager, or your team should use a social media dashboard. A social media dashboard is a desktop application or online service that makes it easier for your business to share posts across the major social media platforms (see Figure 3.13). Examples include Postling, Roost, TweetDeck, and HootSuite. The dashboards show the managed platforms in one browser window, as opposed to switching between browser windows to see Twitter versus Facebook, and so on. Most social media dashboard applications are inexpensive or free and come with management features such as a URL shortener, like ow.ly or bit.ly. These apps shorten your URLs so that they can fit within the character limits of your social media sites (140 characters for Twitter and 420 characters for Facebook).

You also typically find a post scheduler included in a dashboard (see Figure 3.14). This feature enables you to plan posts to various sites. You can write multiple posts and schedule when you want them to appear on your social media sites. By using a post scheduler, you save an enormous amount of time and effort by not having to continuously update your sites, which allows you to focus on other aspects such as responding to customer service posts. For Facebook, many dashboards provide the ability to post to a profile, a Page, or both, so you have posting schedule flexibility.

Another advantage of dashboards is that they separate feeds into customizable columns (see Figure 3.15) By contrast, a standard Facebook account only lets you see one stream of content per account at one time. A dashboard (or social media manager) enables you to manage multiple Facebook accounts.

3.13 A social media dashboard, like this one provided by Hootsuite, allows you to manage multiple social media sites with one application.

3.14 A post scheduler saves an enormous amount of time and enables you to schedule posts on your social media sites.

3.15 A dashboard, like the one shown here in Hootsuite, allows you to see multiple feeds in customizable columns.

The majority of the current dashboard applications cover the big three social media applications — Facebook, Twitter, and LinkedIn — but coverage beyond the most popular social media platforms varies. For example, at this writing, Hootsuite can post to WordPress.*com* blogs, while Tap11 and Postling can post to WordPress.*org.* That detail can be significant if you rely on your blog heavily. To choose, consider how you intend to use other social media alongside Facebook and your website. Also consider which media you use frequently, as some dashboards have convenient sync to other media-sharing sites. For example, TweetDeck supports sharing of photos with Flickr, Twitgoo, and Mobypicture. So depending on your needs and what sites you want to incorporate onto your dashboard, you need to research which dashboard works best for you.

Dashboards provide a number of convenient ways to access information. Nearly all have a mobile app available and some offer e-mail notifications. For example, Postling provides a daily e-mail summary that shows your social media engagement based on keywords you select. This feature is excellent if an e-mail verification is easier for you to review and manage.

If you have a few people maintaining a social media presence for your business, a dashboard can coordinate access for all involved and can be used as a team collaboration tool. Many dashboards enable you to manage all the contacts through various social network accounts. Most dashboards provide immediate communication, and you can send tasks to the members and monitor their progress and responses. This saves time for everyone to focus on other essential activities in your business.

At the same time, be cautious about posting too frequently. The convenience of being able to post across platforms can be *too* convenient, causing you to share repeated posts if the dashboard is not set up correctly. Be sure to map which platforms automatically share with each other when you post, so you don't overwhelm your followers.

Quote, Unquote: The Timing Challenge

"The most difficult approach, to be honest, is scheduling when you'll share new news. It might sound silly, but with six clients, plus our internal needs, our Facebook posting schedule can get filled up fast. So, it becomes a challenge then to figure out a) who are we posting to with this, b) what time are they really going to have their eyes out for this news, and c) who else on Facebook would be interested in seeing this."

— Jerry Sullivan, owner and integrated communication specialist of Framework Media, a social media and PR management firm

Also, some Facebook users are not comfortable with tweets that appear in a Facebook feed because of the hashtags and notations that are frequently used in a tweet. Not everyone understands the Twitter language and the Twitter trends that you may be following, such as #FollowFriday. Be somewhat conscious of this as you set up your posts.

Another helpful aspect of a social media dashboard is the analytics tool, which provides very important information that you can use to determine what to post and when to post on your sites (see Figure 3.16). The analytics tool only analyzes the performance of posts shared from within the dashboard. Many dashboards have begun to combine data from several tools to create comprehensive reports. For example, you can have a report displaying Google Analytics data alongside your Facebook fan Page data.

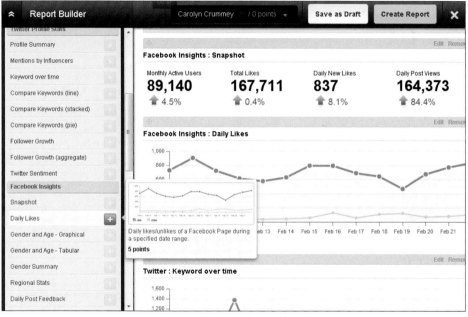

3.16 Analytics from your social media dashboard provide valuable insight to activities on your sites and the response from members.

Dashboards, in short, are great social media management tools for your business. The separate columns can help you focus on your clients in social media and can save time in sending messages, scheduled or otherwise. The gains in efficiency will permit your business to understand which channels provide immediate results from your communication efforts as well as which channels require some adjustment.

Leveraging Offline and Online Marketing

Facebook, as you are now beginning to see, is a very powerful tool to engage your existing customers and find new ones. However, it becomes even more powerful when you use it along with other marketing strategies. For example, maybe you have an event planned for your business. Along with your traditional marketing for this event, such as print and advertising, you can also promote it on your Facebook business Page and group Page. Create it as an event in Facebook and invite your Page followers. You can also post pictures from similar past events so your members can see how fun it will be.

Here's a story of how a hotel used Facebook and a mannequin (yes, just like in the stores) to generate buzz about its business. Scene Marketing Group (www.scenemarketing.net) is the PR and marketing company for the Portland-based Jupiter Hotel. The company's role includes traditional public relations, such as pitching, writing press releases, and managing media relationships as well as digital public relations, such as social media management, blogging, and search engine optimization.

Scene Marketing Group's most successful campaign brought Jupiter Hotel's mascot, Jupiter Lily, to life. A mannequin in the front lobby, Lily was named by the front desk agents after a hotel owner purchased her to showcase T-shirts, sweatshirts, hats, and underwear guests could purchase. The director of marketing, Shannon Pratuch, noticed that guests were snapping pictures of Lily in the lobby and posting them online and bands were leaving her swag and notes. From that came a viral campaign that was launched in January 2010. Facebook is home to Jupiter Lily's profile and the Jupiter Hotel fan Page.

Quote, Unquote: Facebook and Hotel Guests

"Utilizing Facebook as a means to interact with our clientele has provided a targeted niche and means of communicating with guests who are interested in our property as well as return customers. The Jupiter Hotel uses this outlet not only to promote packages and overnight stays but also as a tool for publicizing events; surveying followers for feedback; and sharing imagery, reviews, contests, and more. The fan Page insights program allows our marketing department to test A/B campaigns, flush out trends, research demographics, target our audience and competitor sets, build online awareness, market to feeder cities, and interact with the property's super users on a daily basis."

— Shannon Pratuch, CEO and owner of Scene Marketing Group

As a result of the Jupiter Lily campaign, the number of reservations at the hotel increased significantly. The Jupiter Hotel received many accolades, including the award for Best Social Media in Hospitality in Portland, Oregon by the Social Media Club of Portland. Jupiter Lily was even inducted as an official Radio City Music Hall Rockette in December 2010 with a costume sent from New York City.

Lily is unique because her following online is purely motivated by word of mouth and friends interact with her as a person (see Figure 3.17).

3.17 Jupiter Lily, the mascot of the Jupiter Hotel, has her own Facebook Page with her own set of friends, who interact directly with her as if she were a real person.

| Timeline | Info | Photos | Notes |

Making Money on Facebook

Facebook is a great tool to use to engage your customers by sharing photos and comments. You can start conversations and glean valuable feedback from customers. This engagement is an indirect way that many businesses are making money on Facebook. Facebook can also be a powerful way to generate *direct* revenue for your product or service. By advertising on Facebook, you can reach hundreds, hundreds of thousands, or millions of potential customers.

Making money on Facebook is easy, but if you know some best practices, it's much more profitable.

Selling Online Using Facebook

Selling online, whether through a website, blog, or e-mail newsletter, is pretty easy. You simply showcase your products, market them to your targeted customers, and then enable those customers to buy. Your customers can pay for your product or service through whatever method you choose, whether that is bringing you a pound of apples to your doorstep in exchange for 30 minutes of consulting, paying you through PayPal, or just mailing you a check. However, to maximize your online sales, you need to go beyond the basics and learn the art and science of selling online.

Using Facebook to sell online is no different than any of the other more typical methods. You simply list your products or services, wait for payments, and eke out a living. Or you can take it a step further and learn how to really maximize Facebook for your online sales and boost your e-commerce revenue. This chapter covers how to leverage Facebook to sell products or services online.

Creating a Facebook Page to make money

As I discuss in Chapter 3, your business should create a business Page rather than a group or personal profile Page. If you are using your personal Facebook profile as a business Page, don't.

Before creating your Facebook Page for your business, ensure you have a personal Facebook profile that is fully set up. Use a great photo, fill out all the information, and carefully review and establish the privacy options you are comfortable with.

Business Pages enable multiple administrators. This is great for growing companies with turnover — you can rest assured that if an administrator leaves the company, someone else can still control the Page.

Business Pages are public by default, so they appear on search engine results.

Business Pages are divided into different categories, such as brand, local business, or musician, so they appear in more relevant search results.

With a personal profile, you are required to accept friendship requests. By contrast, anyone can become a fan of your business Page without administrator approval.

Brainstorming content ideas for your Facebook Page

Your Facebook Page is a great way to share content with your followers. The key is providing unique content that encourages followers to continue following your Page. Moreover, Facebook's algorithm for determining which items appear in each user's News Feed takes into account the frequency in which followers of a Page participate by clicking on that Page. This tracking ensures that Page content that is most often clicked on is considered among the top updates listed in News Feeds, where your followers will see it.

Here are some content ideas that you may want to consider for your Facebook Page:

- Pictures of your business at a trade show
- Photos of your business receiving an industry award
- Instructional videos about your product or service. For example, if your product is baked goods, you can post a video on good baking tips in the kitchen.
- Links to articles that your firm contributed to on a relevant site
- Acknowledgments of cherished clients for their contributions to an event
- Preview pictures for upcoming new products and services
- Announcements about upcoming guests on your podcast
- Announcements of upcoming webinars

Adding rich content to your Facebook Page bolsters engagement, and these ideas specifically reinforce the connection your customers and prospective customers have to buy from you again and again.

Using Facebook and Skype

Need to chat with the people who follow you, but don't have enough time to go to their location? Skype and Facebook solved this challenge for you by introducing in-browser Skype integration in Facebook. This enhances your ability to send videos to Facebook friends and contacts and can open new doors of convenience for your business to share information faster and more conveniently. Initiating a call is straightforward. This feature is only available through the reader's personal account (or if they've created a personal Page for their business). You can't call anyone through your business Page.

To start, go to Facebook's video calling start page (www.facebook.com/videocalling) and click Get Started (see Figure 4.1). A pop-up box appears in the lower-right corner of the screen asking you to select a friend to call from the people available in your online chat contacts. This is a quick one-time setup. Once the setup is complete, you're ready to call any of your contacts in Facebook. If your contact isn't online or available for a chat, you can always leave a video message for the contact to see later.

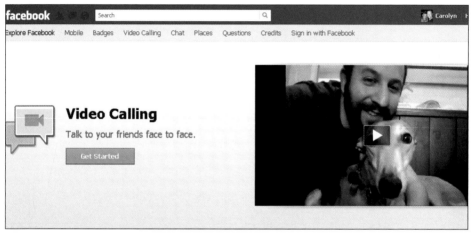

4.1 The Skype integration tool enables you to make video calls directly through Facebook.

To begin a video call, click the video camera icon in a chat window (see Figure 4.2). You can also click the settings button (gear icon) and then click Call in the top-right of your friend's Facebook profile Page when that friend is online.

Facebook/Skype calling works in Internet Explorer, Chrome, Firefox, and Safari.

The Skype integration includes some features that make chat easy and truly beneficial:

- **The time and date of each call you make is listed in your ongoing message history with each friend.** The calls themselves are not recorded or saved.

- **You can continue using chat and other Facebook features during your video call.**

- **You can still use video calling even if you don't have a webcam.** You are able to see and hear your friends, but they are only able to hear you.

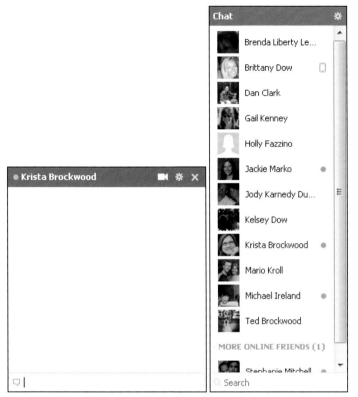

4.2 You can initiate a Skype video call directly from the Facebook chat window.

- **You can make yourself unavailable for calls.** To do so, follow these steps (see Figure 4.3):
  1. **Click the settings (gear) icon on the chat list.**
  2. **Click Go Offline to no longer be available.**
- **If you want to block an individual or a group of individuals from calling or chatting with you, create a block list.** To do this, click the settings (gear) icon in the bottom-right corner of the chat list and choose Advanced Settings. Here you can designate who can and who cannot see you. Additionally, anyone that you unfriend in Facebook is removed from your contact list.

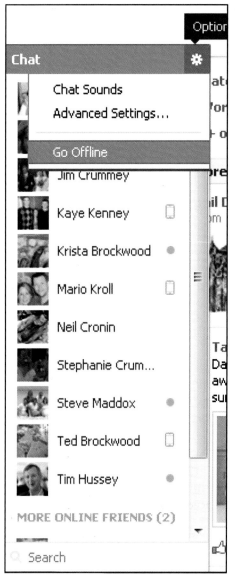

4.3 You can go offline to make yourself unavailable for calls and chats.

You should consider using Skype chat as a way to connect with your clients and followers. You'll find that the service can enhance your relationships by providing an additional means to communicate and follow up with people you have met in the field. You can also leave video messages for those people. Skype integration provides a new channel to communicate with customers, providing a way to make new sales possible. But do note that this only works if you have a personal profile.

Reviewing Your Facebook Page Analytics

Once you create your Facebook Page, it is very important that you regularly monitor the success of the Page. At the very basic, success can be measured by how many people like your Facebook Page, how many users are active, and what posts are most viewed. All these items can be reviewed through your Facebook Page analytics tools.

So to recap, creating your Facebook Page is one of the first steps to selling online. With your Facebook Page, you can post information about the products or services you are selling. You can use analytics to measure how your Page is doing, how effective your content is, and what products generate the most interest. I get more into analytics on Facebook (and in general) in Chapter 3, but I review Facebook's algorithm next.

The Facebook algorithm

When you seek to improve engagement on Facebook, keep in mind the algorithm used to display posts. The algorithm on Facebook, influences how visible a shared post appears on a person's News Feed. This is similar in concept to Google's well-known PageRank algorithm, but it is applied to Facebook rather than Google and is different in the data it considers. A search engine algorithm focuses on the functional processes and design of a website, which can change, but such changes are processed by the algorithm over time. The number of referral links to a website is a factor in the PageRank algorithm, but those links must be picked up by search engines to be incorporated into its calculation (and these referral links can be influenced by other factors of a site).

On the other hand, the Facebook algorithm depends on human activity and newness of that activity. Thus, it is imperative for you to consider your ability to not only monitor Facebook data with more frequency than a web analytics tool, but also to consider the quality of your interactions with followers. The quality affects how your notifications are noticed among followers, which is essential if your intention is to draw people repeatedly to your Page.

Increases in affinity and weight increase your score within the algorithm, while older posts are seen as less valuable than new posts. Affinity is based on the exchange of likes, messages, links, Timeline posts, and comments. The more exchanges that occur around these functions, the better you can influence your rating within the algorithm.

There is no set formula or combination of posts and interactions. There are, however, steps you can take to develop a higher affinity and weight:

- Encourage people to like posts by asking directly. Energize your customers by asking them to participate on your fan Page.

- Post photos, videos, and slides with interesting content to encourage comments from those who respond to sight and sound, as well as provide variety.

- When posting to your site, rather than using a close-ended statement, format your post so that it asks an open-ended question and encourages your followers to interact. The algorithm will account for this interaction and how it exposes your post to a larger audience.

- Gain a sense of when your posts will most likely be seen. Some communication dashboard tools, such as Crowdbooster, suggest times based on past posts.

Insights

If you take the time to follow the steps that you think will increase your affinity and weight in the algorithm, you'll surely want to know if it's having any effect. You can do this by using analytic dashboards such as Facebook Insights. These dashboards are meant to help you manage your communication efforts. The Facebook Insights dashboard (shown in Figure 4.4) provides a single view of all your Facebook analytics related to the following properties:

- Websites that display and use Facebook social plug-ins, such as the Like button.

- Apps, including apps in testing, mobile device, and desktop apps.

- Facebook Pages, including Pages created on Facebook.com and those that are part of the Open Graph protocol, which allows third-party (such as websites and mobiles) connectivity to Faceboook.

As an example, you can view analytics about specific stories that people liked on your website, or how many people commented on your Page posts. This data tells you what your audience finds most interesting so that you can capitalize on that content.

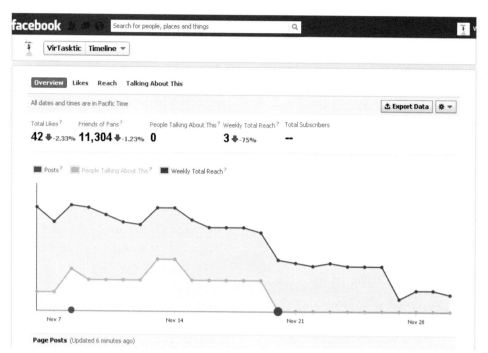

4.4 Facebook Insights gives you great information on the performance of your Page and the interaction of your visitors.

On the Insights dashboard, you can see a variety of metrics and insight about the traffic (or users) visiting your Facebook Page. At the top of the Facebook Insights Page are four sections you can select: Overview, Likes, Reach, and Talking About This.

The Overview section gives you a quick snapshot of total likes, friends of friends (which is how many friends the people had who liked your Page), people talking about this (which is the number of people who interacted with your Page by posting to your Timeline, commenting or other actions), and weekly total reach (which shows you how many people have seen any content related to your Facebook Page).

One of the most important parts of the Overview section is that it shows you the posts in your Page and includes their reach, number of engaged users, number of users talking about this (talking, commenting, or otherwise engaged with a post), and the virality (the percentage of people who have engaged with your post versus someone who has just seen it and not engaged with it).

What I like doing with this section is sorting the posts by one of the metrics (reach, engaged users, talking about this, or virality) and seeing which posts received the highest rankings. This is important so that you know what content was most interesting (or valuable) to your audience. For example, one of my posts, which contained video, had a reach of 342 while a few other posts had reaches of less than 200. My audience (and probably yours, too) likes videos.

Clicking on the Likes section of the Facebook Insights dashboard shows you the gender and age, and countries, cities, and languages of the people who like your Page. You can also see from this area where your likes are coming from — from your Timeline or a Like box or Like button.

Reach is the next metric in Facebook Insights, and it gives you similar demographics to the Likes tab but related to not only who is liking your Page but also to who you are reaching. This section also includes insights in how people see your content. These methods include organic (such as who saw your content in a News Feed), paid (advertising), and viral (someone saw your content or Page through a friend). You can also see the total reach of all three of these methods.

The last section of the Facebook Insights tool is the Talking About This section, where you can see data related to users who are commenting, responding to questions, and other engagement with your Facebook Page. This data only appears if more than 30 people in seven days are talking about your Page.

You can select whether you want to see monthly or weekly data in the top-right corner of the Page. If you select monthly data, the dashboard automatically defaults to the last complete month. If you select weekly data, the dashboard automatically defaults to the last complete week. You can also choose to refine the date range.

Toward the top left of the Facebook Insights Page is a drop-down list with beginning and end dates (see Figure 4.5). If you click this menu, a date range selection appears where you can input the dates whose data you want to see (for example, November 3, 2012 – November 30, 2012).

If at any point you are unsure of what date range you're looking at, you can hover your mouse pointer over the question mark next to the metric and see the options available.

Click Export Data at the top-right corner of the dashboard to export the data. A dialog box asks you to specify the date range for which you want to export data as well as whether you want to get the data as an Excel file or as a CSV (comma separated values) file.

4.5 Facebook breaks down your analytics so you can see specifics about your users and who is interacting with your Page.

Other analytic solutions

There are other analytic solutions available for Facebook that let social media teams focus their scarce time on creating great customer interactions rather than clicking from tool to tool. Many of these provide a means to download data into an Excel spreadsheet, and their range of analytic capabilities centers on communication. Keep in mind that, unlike Facebook Insights, these tools do not focus primarily on Facebook referral sources, thus their scope can differ slightly from what you are looking for. If you are interested in learning more about how the Like button contributes to your Page, Insights may be the more direct way to go. Yet others, like PageLever, provide the same metrics in a more graphic package.

Each of these analytic solutions offers diagnostic utilities that can help guide your social media steps, and all include Facebook Page integration. This is important if you are interested in comparing activity of Twitter versus Facebook, for example. Pricing varies on many of these tools, but most have either a free demo or a free trial. The following sections explain some of the available analytic tools available.

Hootsuite Pro

Hootsuite, the Twitter desktop application available at www.hootsuite.com, provides a dashboard that allows you to see Facebook and Google Analytics and Twitter analytics. Hootsuite enables you to customize the look and feel of this data to show as much or as little of it, from the various social networks, as you want. The analytics dashboard is part of its advanced version of Hootsuite Pro package, which has a low monthly fee.

Crowdbooster

Crowdbooster (www.crowdbooster.com) is a dashboard analytics solution normally used for monitoring Twitter engagement. It also provides measurement of engagement on Facebook Pages. In Crowdbooster, *engagement* is defined by the impressions of a message. Crowdbooster charts the number of impressions with the number of likes. This provides a graphic view of messages that have potentially gained the most reach and response, allowing you to consider eliminating messages that have no significance with followers. Crowdbooster also makes suggestions on which fans are commenting on your Page, thus suggesting who you should follow up with to strengthen your affinity and weight. The dashboard is simpler than most others like Hootsuite in that it does not have a daily breakdown of data and data downloads are not in the free version. The graphs and information provided can be immediately helpful to taking action on your fan Page.

PageLever

Introduced in 2011, PageLever (www.pagelever.com) provides a dashboard for managing multiple Facebook Pages. It breaks its dashboard metrics into three tiers: fan metrics, visibility, and engagement. It highlights key data, such as your Pages' most responsive demographic. It also calculates percentages such as engagement rate, and displays a number of adjustable graphs. This tool provides an additional layer to metrics that appear in Facebook Insights and adds a number of interesting graphs and information. Referral sources, for example, indicate how visitors arrived to your fan Page.

Postling

Postling (www.postling.com) combines a number of share-across-platform features of Hootsuite and TweetDeck and adds delivery of comment summaries to your e-mail, blog post access from within the user interface, and an influence assessment of Twitter followers. With respect to Facebook, Postling can overlay visit data and provide an e-mail summary of your analytics. This platform is more suited for Twitter than Facebook, but it does provide an overview.

Google Analytics

Google Analytics (www.google.com/analytics) is widely used by businesses large and small. As a business intelligence tool, it has helped websites understand their sources of traffic and helped businesses adjust their marketing, be it from search engine optimization, banner ads, pay-per-click ads, content marketing, or offline sources. But there is one specific challenge about its implementation that has plagued business owners with respect to Facebook.

To adjust for this segmentation challenge, Google has modified the solution to better complement how people are discovering sites online. Google introduced a social plug-in feature in version five of Google Analytics. The feature includes social engagement reports that measure how people share content on your site via social actions. Facebook Like button clicks are among these social actions, as well as Google +1 button clicks and Delicious bookmarks. The reports display measurement regarding three kinds of social media–related activity:

- A comparison of the number of Pages viewed per visit, average time on site, bounce rate, and other metrics for visits. This segments data between those who used social actions, which are available on your site, and those who did not.

- A comparison of the number of social actions (+1 clicks, likes, and so on) for each social source and social source–action combination.

- A comparison of the number of actions on each Page of your site with information displayed by social source or by social source–action combination.

The benefit for your business, particularly if a website is its main digital presence, is the capability to assess the effective social media channels worthy of increased investment of engagement and time.

Webtrends Social

Webtrends (www.webtrends.com) is well known for its enterprise-level web analytics. For small businesses, it has introduced Webtrends Social, a dashboard specific to Facebook. It provides a social media management platform to enable marketers to execute, manage, and improve their social media efforts across teams. On Webtrends Social, you can manage your Facebook Timeline, create shareable apps, delegate responses to team members, and analyze your successful efforts. The free version permits one Page, but multiple Pages can be managed for a low monthly fee.

Radian6

Need to listen to your brand? Monitoring brand mentions is the goal of Radian6 (www. radian6.com). Used by advertising agencies, Radian6 is an engagement console that tracks mentions of desired keywords across the web, including Twitter and Facebook. Radian6 provides a monthly subscription that is pricey for the smallest of businesses with the smallest amount of data. It is affordable for those who spend thousands per month on digital advertising. There are also a number of free resources from Radian6, which can be thought starters and are based on the developers' experience.

Adobe Social

Introduced as a limited release beta in March 2011, Adobe Social (www.omniture.com/en/ products/social/social_analytics) monitors and measures popular platforms, including Facebook, YouTube, Twitter, blogs, and forums, so that valuable social data is analyzed in context with all online initiatives. This helps marketers gain answers to potentially correlated data, such as the peak of social sentiment mentions (which is about what people are saying about you in social media)versus peaks in website traffic (which indicates the raw traffic numbers to your website) Adobe Social provides additional analysis for elements of Facebook, such as fan demographics.

Advertising on Facebook

Marketing on Facebook, as you've read, delivers profitable results for your business in two ways: customer interaction and direct advertising. As you work to create advertising that works (it's clicked on and liked) and content that is well received by your audience, keep in mind the exponential effect of Facebook. Not only are you reaching that initial person on Facebook, but through smart advertising and content engagement you are also reaching the friends of your fans. Say you have an audience of 500 fans. If 10 percent of this audience shares your content with their friends, you're reaching 50 more people. If 10 percent of these folks share your content, you're reaching 5 more people. If you get a higher percentage of interaction with your online audience and grow your fan base, your exponential (or multiplier) reach goes even higher.

Another option to effectively sell on Facebook is to use advertising. Facebook ads appear on individuals' Facebook Pages in the right-hand advertising column and in the News Feed. Plus, they link to your Facebook Page or website, which hopefully leads people to purchase your product or service.

Advertising on Facebook is pretty simple and an effective way to do the following:

- **Reach customers.** Target the precise demographic of customers you want to reach.

- **Deepen relationships with customers.** By engaging customers where they spend a lot of their online time, on Facebook, you can engage customers in a variety of interesting ways.

- **Save money.** Big companies can spend lots of money buying a variety of advertisement types: TV, online, print, and so on. As a small-business owner with a small budget, you have few advertising options. Online advertising through Facebook is cost effective, and you only need to spend as much as you want. In this chapter, I have adapted Facebook's effective and simple instructions, which you can access at www.facebook.com/business/ads (see Figure 4.6).

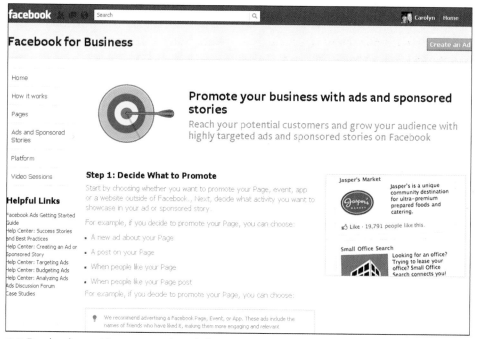

4.6 Facebook provides great tools to help you create ads and makes it a simple step-by-step process.

There are four main steps to create your ad:

1. **Understand Facebook's advertising policies and ad approval process.**
2. **Identify your goals.**
3. **Define who you want to reach with your ad.**
4. **Create your ad and set your budget.**

Before you get started, it is useful to know there are two ways to purchase ads on Facebook:

- Contact Facebook's sales team directly and work with them to find online advertising solutions. This tends to be for large brands with big budgets.
- Buy ads through Facebook's self-serve tool.

The main focus in this book is the self-service tool. When you promote something you've created on Facebook, such as a Page or event, you have the opportunity to show social endorsements in your ad, making it more personally appealing and relevant to your audience.

For example, if you create a Facebook event for a sale or promotion, customers will be able to RSVP to your sale directly from your ad. If a viewer's friend has engaged with the event the viewer will see "Jane Smith and 2 other friends are attending." If someone likes your Facebook Page, a story appears in the News Feed, where his or her friends may also discover your business.

Identifying your goals

The first step to developing an excellent marketing campaign is defining what's most important to you as a business owner. Do you want to increase sales? Generate awareness with a local audience? Promote a specific event? Or get more people to like your Facebook Page?

Your answers to these questions will help shape your goals for your ad campaign:

- What do you want to achieve with your ad?
- Do you want to build awareness of your company, products, services or Facebook Page? Here are some example goals for your campaign:
  - Let people know your company or Facebook Page exists.
  - Increase brand name recognition.
  - Acquire new sales leads that you can follow up with later.

- Do you want to encourage specific actions on your website or on Facebook? If so, here are some example goals for your campaign:

  - Get more people to like your Facebook Page.

  - Get more people to visit your company's website or online store.

  - Increase sales by offering a special discount code for Facebook customers.

The most effective ad campaigns focus on just one goal at a time. For example, to encourage people to visit your store during sale season, you would create an event ad that asks people to RSVP to the sale. This is a very different ad than one you would create to drive traffic to an individual product landing page.

Defining your target customer

Before you launch your campaign, it's important to think about the customers you have and the customers you want to reach in the future.

To identify your audience, ask yourself the following questions about your current customers:

- Who shops in your store, buys from your website, and tells friends about your company or Page today?

- Where are they located? Are they all over the world or in a particular geographic location? Or both?

- Do your customers fit into a specific age range or share an interest in a particular topic?

Creating your advertisement

Create your advertisement with care. Don't rush to create an advertisement and think that sales will explode if you have not taken the time to carefully think about the customers you want to reach with your advertisement, as I explained earlier. The advertisement you create is one of the most important elements to selling online. For a minute, think about the offline advertisements you see throughout the day — hundreds of them — on TV, billboards, magazines, and store windows. Many of them you subliminally ignore, but there are a few, very few, that catch your eye. Facebook advertising is like this, but better. First of all, because you can specifically target your ad to the right profile, the chances of someone being interested in your advertisement are higher. It's also important to be sure that the look and feel of your advertisement is appropriate. For example, there is no need to have a sexy model if you're advertising children's glasses, and you may want to talk about customer service if you're advertising a car dealership.

Facebook has a variety of advertising types, depending on what you want to advertise: a Page, an event, an application on Facebook, or your own website. These ad types are determined when you first create your ad and when you choose the destination of your ad.

To start advertising on Facebook, go to www.facebook.com/advertising or click the Create an Ad link at the very bottom of your Facebook Page.

From here you can select what you want to advertise. This could be an external website address or a Facebook destination ID (such as a Page, app, or event).

You also have the choice to directly pick a Page or Place to advertise or an application or event. In this example, I am going to choose a Page.

You're now presented with three options:

- **Get More Page Likes.** This helps you build a bigger audience.
- **Promote Page Posts.** This helps you get people to see and engage with a post that's important.
- **See Advanced Options.** You can work on some more advanced advertising options such as cost per click.

For now, just focus on building a bigger audience for your existing Facebook Page.

Step one: Design your ad

Your ad is made up of a title, ad body copy, and an image (see Figure 4.7).

In this step you develop the headline and body of your advertisement, choose where people will land when they click on your advertisement (Timeline or photo), and upload an image.

- **Title.** Grab attention! You have 25 characters, including spaces, to capture people's interest.
- **Body.** In 135 characters or less, describe the benefits of your product or service. If you want people to click through your ad to take specific action, be sure to call that out with simple, active language, like "Learn more now."

A few tips to help you:

- The most successful ads on Facebook include images that are clear, easy to spot, and directly related to the content of your ad.
- When designing your ad, think about your advertising goals and how the ad can help support them. For example, if you're looking to drive foot traffic to your

business, use the ad title and ad body copy to tell your customers why they should visit your store.

* You see a preview of your ad as you create it, allowing you to make adjustments. The preview can save you time when you submit your ad for approval, enabling you to catch concerning errors before Facebook processes the ad and runs it. Take great care during this process, as it can lend heavily to the success or failure of your ad. Also, to avoid common pitfalls, review Facebook's advertising guidelines at http://www.facebook.com/ad_ guidelines. php, which review the do's and don'ts of advertising on Facebook.

4.7 The Facebook ad creation tool walks you through each of the steps needed to begin creating your ad.

To make your ad more successful, it's important to target the ad to reach only the people who would find the ad copy most compelling. For example, say you own a yogurt shop. Your customers fall into three main groups: students from the local college, people who live within walking distance, and parents who drive across town to bring their kids to your family-friendly atmosphere. You could create three ads, each with slightly different goals, to target each of these groups.

In Figure 4.8, the ad on the left targets students, focusing on student discounts and late-night hours. The ad in the middle targets parents who live within the same city as your shop, mentioning special prices for children and playdates. The ad on the right targets people who might frequent the shop, promoting flavors of the week and new products.

4.8 You can create three different ads for the same product to target specific groups.

Step two: Use Sponsored Stories

Next you need to decide if you want to advertise using Sponsored Stories. Using Sponsored Stories helps friends of those who already like your business's Page discover the Page you are advertising. You can remove Sponsored Stories (not use it) or keep the People liking your Page check box selected.

Step three: Select your audience

In this area you can select the geographic location in which your advertisement will run. If you are only focusing on building an audience for your Gilbert, Arizona donut shop, then just advertise to visitors who live near Gilbert, Arizona. When choosing your audience you can also select your audience by age and gender. Face it, a 13-year-old child is different than a 45-year-old adult. Precisely target your advertisement to the demographic that's relevant. In this step you can also select broad interest categories of your audience based on what they do (their interests), their family status, the mobile device they use, and more. The last two advertising options in this step are important as well. Connections — do you want to advertise to everyone or just to those people connected to your Page? Or maybe you want to refine your advertising even more and only advertise to folks whose friends are connected to your Page.

As shown in Figure 4.9, you can target people based on specific characteristics.

4.9 Facebook allows you to be very specific in the demographic of who your ad will reach.

- **Location.** By city, state, province, zip code, or country. You must select at least one country.

- **Demographics.** By age range, gender, or a specific language, which is available under the See Advanced Targeting Options link. Within the advanced options you can also filter by gender, interest, and relationship.

- **Likes and interests.** What are your customers' hobbies or passions? Unlike search advertising, where you target the words people search for, on Facebook you can target people by their interests. For example, if you sell cameras you could specify that you want your ad displayed to people interested in photography. You can add multiple likes and interests to reach a broader section of people.

- **Education and work.** You can direct your campaign to students in a specific college or people with a particular level of education by choosing this selection under the See Advanced Targeting Options link.

As you change your targeting preferences, note that the total number of people who might see your ad changes. For the most impact, it's best to target your ad to a small, focused audience while making sure that the group is large enough to have a positive impact.

Audience Targeting Tip

What are your customers' hobbies or passions? Unlike search advertising, where you target the words people search for, on Facebook you can target people by their interests. For example, if you sell cameras you could specify that you want your ad displayed to people interested in photography. You can add multiple interests to reach a broader section of people.

Step four: Name your campaign and set your pricing

After you complete the selections for targeting your ad, step 4 of the process is naming your campaign and establishing a budget (see Figure 4.10). This step is pretty straightforward. My recommendation is that you set a moderate daily campaign budget ($10–50 per day) and test your online advertisement. As you see it working, increase your advertising spend appropriately. If it's not working the way you like, then adjust the campaign until you see the results you like.

A *campaign* is an ad or group of ads that share a daily budget and schedule. After you create your first ad, you can create more ads for the same campaign or create new campaigns. There are two types of campaigns that you can run:

- **Cost per click (CPC).** This is a type of campaign pricing where you pay each time someone clicks on your ad. This is the best type of campaign to use when you want to drive specific action on your website or Facebook Page.

- **Cost per thousand impressions (CPM).** In this type of campaign pricing, you pay based on the number of people who view your ad. This is the best type of campaign pricing to use to raise general awareness within a targeted audience.

Step five: Review and submit your ad

To preview your ad or review other details, click Review Ad at the bottom of the Campaigns, Pricing, and Scheduling page. If you need to change any of the details of the ad, click Edit Ad at the bottom of the page. You can change your title, body copy, image, or destination URL. When you're satisfied with your ad, type your payment information and then click Place Order.

At this point, if you don't already have a Facebook account, you'll be guided through a process. You'll use your Facebook account to manage the ad you've just created.

3. Campaigns, Pricing and Scheduling   Ad Campaigns and Pricing FAQ

Account Currency

US Dollar (USD)

Account Time Zone

Country/Territory   United States

Time Zone   (GMT-08:00) Pacific Time

Campaign & Budget

Campaign Name: My Ads

Budget (USD):   50.00   Per day   [?]

What is the most you want to spend per day? (min 1.00 USD)

Schedule

Campaign Schedule: ☑ Run my campaign continuously starting today

Pricing

Based on your targeting options, Facebook suggests a bid of **$0.65** per click. You may pay up to this much per click, but you will likely pay less.
Note: Tax is not included in the bids, budgets and other amounts shown.

Set a Different Bid (Advanced Mode)

Review Ad   ✉ Questions about creating your ads?

Facebook © 2012 · English (US)   About · Advertising · Create a Page · Devel

4.10 Creating your campaign name and budget is a very important step in ad creation.

Congratulations. You've created your very first advertisement on Facebook (or made a current one better). It's also important that you manage your advertising budget and track your performance so you know if the advertisements are working and then work to improve your advertisements.

Determining cost and budgeting

There are many critical components in regard to advertising that you need to get right to ensure your Facebook advertisement is more than a pretty icon on a computer screen, and that it leads to sales. The amount you pay for your advertisement is important in determining the profitability of your advertising campaign. For example, if you pay $5 per click for an advertisement and get 10,000 clicks, your advertisement will cost $50,000. If only 100 of those who clicked bought a $10 item from you, then your revenue from the advertisement is $1,000. You are losing $49,000 on each set of ads. It is important that you measure your advertisement to know what is the best price to pay for it so you make the most profit per click.

Daily budget, daily spend limit, and lifetime budget

You have complete control over how much you spend daily. The ad budget that you set for a new campaign is your *daily budget*. It represents the maximum amount that you are willing to spend on that campaign each day you are advertising. Your ads automatically stop showing once your budget has been met for the day. You can change your daily campaign budget, or pause or delete your ads from within your Ads Manager at any time.

When you log in to Facebook, scroll to the bottom of the Page and click the advertising link to go to Faceboook's campaign manager. I found it a bit hard to click this link as some Facebook Pages are very long. Another solution is to go to www.facebook.com/advertising and click the advertising link on the bottom of this Page.

Keep in mind that your daily budget is different from your daily spend limit. The *daily spend limit* is the limit Facebook sets to manage payments, and it automatically increases as you successfully make payments at previous limits. It's similar to a credit rating. *Available impressions* are the number of impressions or views that your advertisement has available to it based on your targeting. *Winning bids* are the maximum cost per click you agree to pay, which affects how often your advertisements are shown. The limit is reset at midnight in your select time zone each day. Your daily spend limit increases automatically as you successfully make payments. However, you will never pay more than the sum of your maximum daily budgets.

Similar to your daily budget, your *lifetime budget* is the amount you are willing to spend over the full lifetime of your advertising campaign on Facebook. The total you spend on your Facebook ad campaign will not exceed this amount.

You may also change these settings in your Ads Manager after you set your ad live. You'll notice the Duration is editable in your campaign settings. Each ad within a campaign is delivered based on these settings.

In the Facebook Ads Manager (which as of this writing is changing), click on the campaign you want to edit. At the top of the Page is a column for budget. Click the pen icon next to the dollar amount to display edit budget and schedule. Here you can edit the daily budget of your advertisement campaign and the campaign's lifetime budget using the drop-down list. You can also edit the campaign schedule in this area as well.

Auction system

Facebook ads work on an auction-based bidding system, which means the market sets the price of your ad. When you set a maximum bid, you are saying that you are willing to pay up to that bid price per click or per thousand views of your ad.

Here's how it works: Your max bid competes against other advertisers' bids to determine which ad gets displayed to the target audience and how much you ultimately pay (up to your max bid, and never in excess of your daily budget).

If you're trying to reach a highly desirable audience during a particularly popular part of the day, you are more likely to have to pay your maximum bid for each click or impression.

Facebook can help you select the right bid amount for your advertisement or you can make your own bid choices by selecting advanced mode (see the Advanced Mode link in the Campaigns, pricing and scheduling section of the advertisement-creation tool).

The suggested bid range shows you the range of bids that are currently winning the auction among ads similar to yours. It is recommended to set a bid price within or above the suggested pricing range provided for your ad. Your maximum bid is the most you'll pay for a click on your ad or per thousand impressions delivered depending on whether you choose to pay per click (CPC) or per thousand impressions (CPM). Facebook only charges the amount that is required for your ad to win the auction, which may be lower than your maximum bid.

Test different messages and images

After running these ads for a while, you can start to refine the messaging, images, and offers to see what works best with each customer group. You may also start to branch out and try to reach new audiences.

The Like button in Facebook advertisements

Many Facebook ad types have a Like button. Like is a familiar action Facebook users use to attribute value to various objects on the site — photos, Timeline posts, status updates, and notes. By clicking Like, users express their sentiment about your business or organization and share this expression with their friends. When users like your business or organization, their friends can see that action in their version of the ad. The Like button only appears in your ad if you are promoting a Facebook object such as a Page, application, or event.

When you hover over an advertisement that is displaying in Facebook an X appears in the top right of the advertisement. When you click this advertisement you have two options: hide the advertisement or hide all advertisements related to this advertisement. The X is a way users can give Facebook quick and easy feedback on the ads they see. Facebook takes this feedback into account as it improves its advertising system for all advertisers and users.

Using the Facebook Ads Manager

Creating an advertisement on Facebook and properly targeting it is only half the work. The real work is measuring the effectiveness of your advertisement. Facebook's Ads Manager is a powerful tool you can use to measure the effectiveness of your advertisement (see Figure 4.11).

4.11 Facebook Ads Manager monitors specific information about your campaigns so you can determine their success.

Facebook Ads Manager has three main displays that appear when you first examine a specific campaign:

- **The Audience graph.** This graph shows you how many people your ads reached compared to your total targeted audience in the last 28 days. To reach more of your potential audience, try raising your bids and budgets. Mouse over each circle to see the number of people included in each set. Hover over the question marks to see the definition of each metric.

- **Response.** Metrics help you understand the performance of your Facebook ads and Sponsored Stories, and how your audience has responded to your message. This data is updated constantly, so you can measure real-time results and quickly adapt your campaigns to be more successful.

- **Ad management.** When you click on an ad in your Ads Manager, the details for that ad appear within the table, so you never have to leave the Page.

Measuring advertising success

As with any advertising, you can use a variety of metrics to measure your Facebook ads. With Facebook, you can measure how many people your advertisement has the potential to reach based on your target audience. You can also review demographic results for your campaign and the number of people who saw your advertisement. This section looks at some ways to measure your audience.

The metrics in the Ads Manager can help you determine how well your ad campaign is doing. If you have used Google AdWords or Microsoft adCenter, you are in luck — the details for running a CPC campaign in Facebook will be second nature with only a few differences.

Facebook ads operate a bit differently than most other cost-per-click ads. The most significant difference is the keyword algorithm that determines when an ad appears. Most cost-per-click networks base the appearance of their ads on the keywords the viewer uses in a search query. Thus, the mind-set of the visitor is based on eliminating a task, finding information, or resolving a certain problem. If your ad is for attracting customers looking for apples, then your ad has to cover apples as a keyword, be it Red Delicious or Edith Smith. When you first create your ad (www.facebook.com/advertising) or using the Ads Manager after your advertisement is created, you can edit keywords that people are interested in and that trigger whether your advertisement is seen. In Ads Manager, click on the campaign you want to edit. In the resulting screen, which has more details about the campaign, click on the campaign, and the screen opens up to provide more detailed editing options.

Facebook ads are targeted based on the likes and interests listed in users' profiles. This means that ads are not shown from a search, but based on activity of the audience. Using the apple example (if you are not too hungry by now), a Facebook ad for your apples would display next to baking contests, cookouts, and recipe tips, rather than content or user profiles interested in ice hockey, watch collections, or scuba diving This makes Facebook ads a more interesting marketing tactic for your business — you have to consider how and why someone would use your offering. If you have constructed a good business model, you should be able to think of those events and plan to insert those keywords into your Facebook ad.

An *impresssion* is the number of times your ad is shown as an aggregate. Impressions are part of the calculation for the CPM (cost per thousand impressions) and indicate the range in which the ad is shown in a network. In addition to impressions, other metrics to use in your analysis of ads (and Sponsored Stories) include the following:

- **Clicks.** The number of times someone clicks on the link provided in an ad.
- **Click-through rate (CTR).** This is the ratio of clicks to impressions.

- **Price.** The average amount you are paying per click (CPC) or per 1,000 impressions (CPM).

- **Social CTR.** The number of social clicks received divided by the number of social impressions.

- **Social impressions.** Impressions that were shown with the names of the viewer's friends who liked your Page, RSVP'd to your event, or used your app. If you're not advertising a Page, event, or app, you won't see social data.

- **Social reach.** People who saw your ad with the names of their friends who liked your Page, RSVP'd to your event, or used your app. If you're not advertising a Page, event, or app, your ad won't have social reach.

- **Social percentage.** The percentage of impressions where your ad was shown with the names of the viewer's friends who liked your Page, RSVP'd to your event, or used your app. If you're not advertising a Page, event, or app, you won't see social data.

- **Spent.** The amount you spent during the selected period.

- **Targeted audience.** The approximate number of people your ads or Sponsored Stories can reach based on your targeting. With 1 billion active users on Facebook, you can target the precise people who are most likely to be interested in your business or brand.

- **Reach.** The number of real people who saw your ads or Sponsored Stories. Facebook makes it easy for businesses to talk to real people through highly targeted ads and Sponsored Stories. Reach is different than impressions, which include people viewing an ad multiple times.

- **Frequency.** The average number of times people saw your ad.

- **Connections.** The number of people who liked your Facebook Page, RSVP'd to your event, or installed your app within 24 hours of seeing an ad. If you're not advertising a Page, event, or app, you won't see Connections data.

Ad performance reporting in Ads Manager

There are three summary reports that capture the aforementioned metrics. These reports can be exported to an Excel sheet, which is perfect if you have an advanced analytics team importing data into a custom dashboard. Reports can be e-mailed to you if you need just a periodic summary. You can select the duration, the period for your campaign. Your choices include Last 7 days, Today, Yesterday, Last 28 days, and custom duration for specific time lengths. Each report can be displayed by campaign, ad, or even Pages if your social media team is managing a multiple Pages.

On the left side of the Ads Manager, click in reports. Then select the parameters of your report type and click the Generate Report button.

These are the five reports:

- **Advertising Performance.** This report covers impressions, clicks, click-through rate (CTR), and spend.

- **Responder Demographic.** This report provides valuable demographic information about users who see and click on your ads. After reviewing this report, you will be better able to optimize your filters for targeting your audience.

- **Actions by Impressions Time.** This report shows the number of conversions on your Page over time (that is, 0–24 hours, 1–7 days, or 8–28 days).

- **Inline Interactions.** If user engagement is very important to you, this report gives you insight into the performance of ads or Sponsored Stories for Page posts.

- **News Feed.** This report shows how Sponsored Stories perform in the News Feed, including the average position within the feed where the story was inserted.

First ad analysis steps

First, establish a baseline performance for your ads. This is particularly useful if you plan to run ads on occasion for your business, promotion, or Page. Gaining a sense of how well your ad does in an initial run can indicate what improvements or changes to the ads are necessary.

You can then use that baseline information to test different aspects of the ad that increase a metric of interest. Maybe you need a higher CTR for a particular region or demographic. Having a baseline and then running a test can help you focus your next efforts.

You can compare the CPC and CPM data from your ads. The one that registered the lowest among these metrics provides the best cost performance for clicks and impressions shown. But you can get more specific than this. Use each of these reports to gain some segmentation perspective of your ad by time. For example, maybe women are more active users of your Facebook Page at night. Maybe 20-year-old males interested in animals are more active users of your Page in the morning. Advertising is great, but being able to segment your audience by demographics and their interaction with your Facebook Page is critical.

The Ads Manager provides ways to match your ad performance with demographics that complement your business model. Through responder demographics, you can develop answers to the following questions:

- Which segments give the best CTR? It is possible that some demographics are responding to your ads better than others?

- Is the response for the demographic better or worse than you had expected? If you created a baseline, you can see if the ad run at full tilt performed as expected. This is particularly helpful when testing one ad combination versus another.

One mistake some businesses make with cost-per-click ads is to run them continuously in the same manner that an ad typically appears in a newspaper. CPC ads can certainly be run that way, but they are meant for more targeted audiences. This is especially true in light of how Facebook displays ads. Running continuously without periodic review can waste advertising budget. You have a rare opportunity to be more targeted with Facebook, so take advantage of it! If you have a constrained ad budget, consider cost-per-click and cost-per-impression advertising as a "turbo boost" to your Facebook presence or overall digital marketing plan.

Remember that images may be unique to Facebook ads over other CPC ads, but so is image fatigue. Images can play a factor in a Facebook user's decision to click on an ad. The viewer of your ad will have spent a lot of time on Facebook — Mashable reported in 2010 that the average Facebook user spends more than seven hours *daily* on the social network. So chances are they may see your ad repeatedly throughout the time the ad runs. This can mean a number of impression opportunities for the ad to be memorable, but it also means those same people can end up feeling that they have seen the ad too much if the ad picture does not change.

Also keep in mind that a landing page is still valuable for a Facebook ad, just like a CPC or banner ad. (A *landing page* is a web page on which your customers arrive when they click on the ad.) Your ads are a lead in for the action you want customers to do on the landing page.

Many businesses link their ads directly to their websites. That is not the best practice in a number of cases, particularly when a web page can have multiple pieces of information that can make a call to action too confusing. E-commerce sites and blogs can have this problem. A landing page has content that is directly related to your ad. Make sure there are no pop-up pages that occur when someone lands on your landing page. If the landing page is a gateway to your site, make sure its appearance matches or mimics your main website for a coherent look.

Remember that you can budget for Facebook ads and a CPC ad in another network. That may sound super basic but can be worthwhile to give two different avenues for having your business discovered. Likes and interests are different than a search query, and most importantly, the purpose for an ad is to make your business, product, service, or event discoverable.

A Page, event, or app allows people to connect with your business in many ways throughout Facebook. Ads help create awareness of your business' Facebook presence. Connections tells you how many people connected with your business after seeing your ads, even if they didn't click, so you know you're driving results.

As you can see, there is a lot of data you can view and analyze in regard to your Facebook advertisement. Maybe you don't have time to manage your advertisement, but ensure that someone does. Consider the frequency of your ad campaign to evaluate whether you are broadcasting your message with the right intensity or need to make changes to your marketing strategy. The only thing worse than advertising is investing the money to advertise and not taking the time to measure the effectiveness of that advertising to improve it.

Using Sponsored Stories

Facebook has a variety of methods you can use to market your business to new customers and engage existing customers. Beyond paid advertising and creating an engaging Page with content, Sponsored Stories takes the natural interaction someone makes on your Page or application and promotes this on the right column of their friends' Facebook Page (see Figure 4.12) or News Feed.

Why is this important? Normally when someone interacts with your brand on Facebook that interaction is placed on their friends' News Feeds. However, those stories are usually only seen if they are visible to users at the time they are on Facebook. Over time, new stories appear on top, pushing down older ones. Sponsored Stories solve this problem by making your users' interactions more visible. Choosing to run a Sponsored Story along with your ad campaign optimizes your marketing reach. You do not, however, have to run them together and can run just one or the other.

There are seven types of Sponsored Stories. Select the right one for you based on your goals and the source of the stories you want to amplify: your Facebook Page, Facebook place (for customers to check in), your website, or Facebook app.

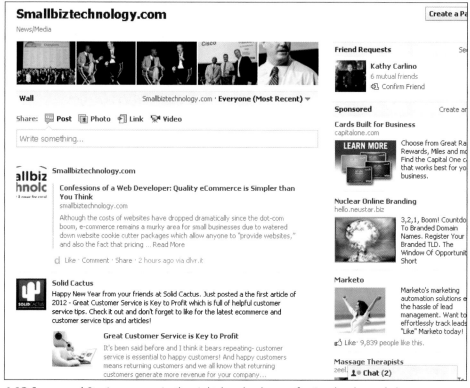

4.12 Sponsored Stories appear in the right-hand column of a Facebook user's home page and in the News Feed.

Here are some examples:

- **Acquire more fans.** Let others know that their friends are liking your Page.
- **Engage with more of your fans.** Show your posts to a wider audience.
- **Drive in-store traffic.** Let others know when their friends check in to your location.
- **Increase app engagement.** Let others know who is using or sharing your app or game.

Creating a Sponsored Story

To create a Sponsored Story, you follow many of the same steps as you do when creating an ad:

1. **To create a Sponsored Story, go to** www.facebook.com/advertising **and click Create an Ad.** You must log into Facebook if you are not already logged in.

2. **Select what you want to advertise from the list: either a Facebook destination (your Page) or an external URL.**

3. **Click Promote Page Posts in the "What would you like to do" section of the advertising creation page.**

4. **Choose the post on your Page you wish to promote (see Figure 4.13).** You can also set this so Facebook automatically promotes the most recent post, as opposed to you manually selecting one particular post to promote.

   a. If you click Show Advanced Options, you'll be presented with an option to add tracking tags to URLs included in your promoted posts. Tracking tags are used to better track the effectiveness of your promoted posts campaign.

5. **Select how your promoted posts are shown in Sponsored Stories.** Your promoted posts can be shown to the friends of people who

   a. like your Page post

   b. comment on your Page post

   c. share your Page post

6. **Choose your audience.** You can specify a geographic location by zip code, state, or country. You can also specify age range, gender, precise interests, and overall broad categories of the person who should be shown your promoted post.

   The Connections options is very powerful and allows you to granularly show your promoted posts only to people who have a certain connection to your Page or post. Click See Advanced Targeting Options to see even more detailed selection options.

7. **Set your campaign name, price, and schedule.** Feel free to refer to the overall advertising steps for fuller details on this stage.

4.13 Sponsored Stories are another way to advertise your business and are very easy to set up.

8. **Click Review Ad.**

9. **When you are finished reviewing your ad, click Place Order.**

If you've already set up your ad and wish to change it, you can simply go into the Ads manager to pause or delete your ad and then re-create a Sponsored Story campaign.

Setting up your budget and targeting criteria

Sponsored Stories are only seen by friends of people who engage with your Facebook Page. Using the traditional advertising targets, you can further segment who you reach with parameters such as location and gender. Setting the budget for a Sponsored Story is very similar to doing it for any other advertisement. As you select bids, don't select them too low or your advertisements won't show. Set them within or above the suggested ranges.

Generating more stories about your business

Sponsored Stories are very powerful and are a great way for your audience members to tell their friends about your business. To make Sponsored Stories as effective as possible, make sure you do things that cause your audience to take action, such as the following:

- To build interest in people liking your Page, purchase Facebook advertisements. Bolster your campaign by using Page Like Stories to amplify these actions on Facebook.

- Make sure you don't leave your website out of the mix. Encourage your website visitors to like your website and send a link to their friends using Facebook's variety of social plug-ins. You can also amplify these actions with Sponsored Stories.

In summary, Sponsored Stories provide a layer on top of your Facebook advertising effort. If you find your traditional Facebook advertising a success, Sponsored Stories can help your brand (or product or service) build much deeper engagement with your audience and the friends of your audience.

There is also an app made by Wildfire called Storyteller, which is meant to add additional nuance to Sponsored Stories. The Storyteller app is designed to turn user feedback and opinions into not just News Feed stories but also Sponsored Stories. You can add an app link to your Facebook Pages, on which you ask fans to answer a question or provide an opinion. Users can then share those answers with their Facebook friends and post it on their Timelines or have the comments appear as a Sponsored Story on their Facebook Pages.

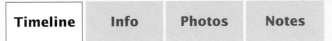

chapter 5

Timeline Info Photos Notes

Boosting Your Website with Facebook

Sometimes my head spins with all the options small businesses have for online engagement. At first you had just websites to worry about. Then blogging was all the rage. Now social media has come of age and everyone is telling you to engage with social media, which is why you are reading this book. It can be confusing.

This chapter shows you how to leverage the power of Facebook and your website, which are even more powerful when blended. It is not an either/or proposition: You typically can't do away with your website and just maintain a Facebook Page. And you can't afford not to be on Facebook and focus only on your website. This chapter shows you how to encourage customers to engage with your website through Facebook.

Integrating Facebook with Your Blogs and Website

Your overall online presence is critical and may be the most important part of finding new customers and keeping the ones you have. Word of mouth is important, but in 2012, a business's online presence is more powerful.

For many businesses, a website is one of the most important tools for forming this online presence. Your website alone is powerful, but what's even more powerful is integrating Facebook with your blog or website. This integration could be as simple as linking to your website from your Facebook Page or writing on your blog about a photo on your Facebook Page. The integration could be as complicated as enabling your Facebook users to log in to special sections of your website through their Facebook accounts. You could also integrate your blog's discussion boards with Facebook.

Facebook is a very powerful marketing tool, and smart businesses think of ways to integrate and leverage it with their websites and blogs.

First, here are a few tips from Jeff Bullas, a digital marketing and social media strategies expert. He wrote nine ways to integrate your website and Facebook in his blog, some of his steps include the following:

- Use Facebook to drive traffic to your website and blog (see the J.Crew link in Figure 5.1).
- Use Facebook to drive traffic to the company blog(s) by linking to the article in a Facebook update (see Figure 5.2).
- Link to your other social media sites on your Facebook Page (see Figure 5.3).

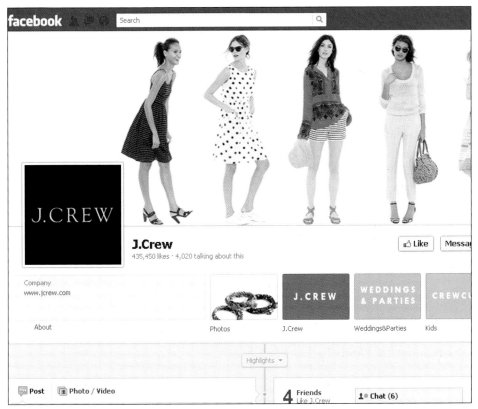

5.1 Creating an obvious link back to your website encourages users to click and visit your site.

5.2 Integrating your blog into your Facebook Page encourages more views from visitors and fans.

5.3 You should always provide links to your other social media sites on your Facebook Page.

- Integrate your e-mail sign-up form on your Facebook Page (see Figure 5.4).

- Provide content on your Facebook Page that incentivizes users to visit your blog or website (see Figure 5.5).

- Offer specials on your Facebook store that link to your e-commerce store (see Figure 5.6).

5.4 Inviting visitors to join your e-mail list when they come to your site increases your marketing reach and allows additional interaction with the user.

TIP

You can also use apps to more easily manage your e-mail list. One example is ContactMe (www.contactme.com).

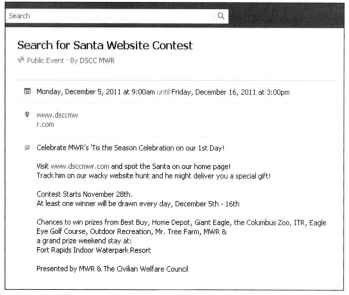

5.5 By creating a competition that drives traffic back to your website, you should see a large increase in website traffic.

Facebook has made it easier than ever to implement social media sharing into your website and blog by developing applications and plug-ins that simplify the connection process. By working with a smart web developer, you can now more closely integrate your website content with the world of your Facebook audience.

In July 2008, Facebook launched Facebook Connect, enabling users to interact more deeply with your website or blog. Facebook Connect gave developers a way to integrate the Facebook platform beyond Facebook.com. Essentially, visitors to your website could now log in or sign in to your website by using their Facebook login information. By connecting in this manner, your users had decided to share their personal information directly with your website and make it known to their friends in Facebook that they connected directly with your site.

5.6 Use your Facebook Page to increase sales and drive visitors back to your e-commerce store.

Quote, Unquote: Facebook and Open Graph

"The Open Graph protocol enables you to integrate your web pages into the social graph. It is currently designed for web pages representing profiles of real-world things — things like movies, sports teams, celebrities, and restaurants. Including Open Graph tags on your web page makes your page equivalent to a Facebook Page. This means when a user clicks a Like button on your page, a connection is made between your page and the user. Your page will appear in the Likes and Interests section of the user's profile and you have the ability to publish updates to the user. Your page will show up in the same places that Facebook Pages show up around the site (e.g., search), and you can target ads to people who like your content. The structured data you provide via the Open Graph protocol defines how your page will be represented on Facebook."

Source: http://developers.facebook.com/docs/opengraphprotocol.

In 2010, Facebook began to transition away from the Facebook Connect brand because underlying technologies are the same regardless of what you are building: apps, websites, or programs on devices. Though most of the Facebook Connect functionality is still available, Facebook has renamed this process Open Graph (see Figure 5.7).

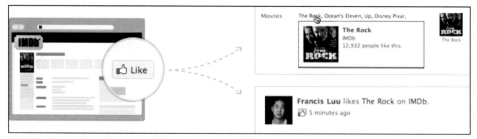

5.7 The Open Graph protocol shares activity richly across Facebook. When someone likes your website by clicking the Like button, that information is instantly shared to the linking Facebook Pages and user Pages.

Connecting your users' accounts with Facebook accounts

If you want to increase the interaction on your website, you can install the Login plug-in, which allows visitors to log in, or sign in, to your site using their Facebook information. This process pulls the visitors' information from their Facebook profiles after an authentication process and eliminates the need to complete additional registration forms. You can access the Login plug-in at https://developers.facebook.com/docs/reference/plugins/login.

You have two options to connect your website with users: the original Login button (see Figure 5.8) or the newer Login button with faces. Unlike the original Login button, the newer button shows profile pictures of the user's friends who have already signed up for your site, in addition to a Login button (see Figure 5.9). While the function of both buttons is the same, those using the new button with faces have a higher conversion rate, so I suggest you use this button on your website, which you do by selecting the Show Faces check box.

To complete the code, choose the width of the plug-in and, if you choose to Show Faces, the maximum rows of photos you want displayed.

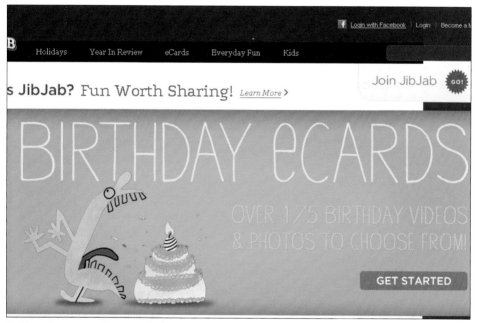

5.8 You have two choices of what type of Login button to display. I suggest using the button that shows faces for a higher conversion rate.

Login to IMDb ×

Login with your IMDb account

e-mail or ID:

Password:

Login! Forgot your password?

More login options

Login with Google

Login with Facebook

Mario Kroll, Dan Clark and 3 friends are using IMDb.

Need an account?

Registering with IMDb is free! Please see our registration page or use your Facebook account to log in.

5.9 The newer Login with Facebook button with faces allows your visitors to see their friends who have already signed up or registered with your website.

Connecting accounts can be completed when a user logs in to Facebook from your site or accepts a connect invitation request from an already connected friend (see Figure 5.10).

Carolyn DeWolf Crummey
Tuesday

Share your latest and greatest photos on Photobucket!

Join me on Photobucket!
register.photobucket.com

Photobucket offers image hosting, free photo sharing and video sharing. Upload your photos, host your videos, and share them with friends and family.

Join Photobucket · via Photobucket

Like · Comment

5.10 When visitors sign up on your website through the Login with Facebook app, they are given the opportunity to invite their friends to visit and log in to your site.

Your website and blog are powerful tools for publishing content beyond just selling a product. Working with a developer to leverage the power of Facebook and engage your online visitors where they are already engaged (Facebook) is very compelling.

Authenticating users

When visitors to your website choose to sign up using Login with Facebook, they go through an authentication process. Three things happen in this process:

- Facebook authenticates users to ensure that they are who they say they are.

- Facebook authenticates your website to ensure that the users are giving their information to your site and not to someone else.

- The users must explicitly authorize your website to access their information to ensure that they know what data they are disclosing to your site.

While this may seem like a daunting process, it is not. The user only needs to click a button to go through authentication, and the program running in the background of the application ensures the transfer and authorization of all necessary information.

For example, when visitors come to your website and click Login with Facebook, a dialog box appears requesting their permission to access information (see Figure 5.11). By clicking Allow, the user completes the entire process of authentication and authorization.

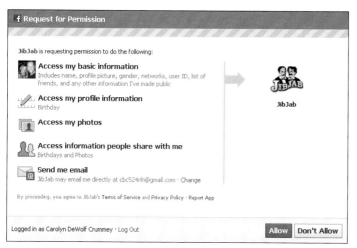

5.11 After choosing to log in with Facebook, the user must first allow the site to access certain information to go through the authentication process.

You can show your visitors additional dialog boxes that encourage more interaction after they sign in or register with your website. For example, you can ask them to sign up for daily alerts or newsletters by providing an e-mail address (see Figure 5.12).

5.12 Asking your visitor for an e-mail address for a daily alert or newsletter is an additional way to interact and increase your marketing capability with the user.

Another option is to ask users to invite their Facebook friends to visit your site and register or sign in. With this option, users simply click a friend's name or multiple friends' names (see Figure 5.13). After choosing those they want to invite, an invitation is sent directly to the recipient through Facebook (see Figure 5.14). This invitation appears in the News Feed on the recipient's Page where all of that user's friends can see the invitation and the link to your website.

5.13 Adding a box that asks users to invite their friends to join your website is a great way to increase your marketing reach.

5.14 An invitation is sent to all recipients chosen with a direct link back to your website.

NOTE If the recipient of an invitation has set security settings to disallow this type of posting, the invitation does not appear in his or her News Feed.

Publishing News Feed stories

Publishing News Feed stories is a way to integrate your content across your site and Facebook. It can be a timesaver when updating your online presence, because the content on your website is also published on the web.

One way to publish New Feed stories is through Facebook Connect or Open Graph. Depending on a user's login state and authorization of Facebook information on your site, there are three possibilities:

- If the user has authorized Facebook and is logged in, you can publish one-line stories automatically, or you can implement feed forms to allow your users to post short or full stories.

- If the user is logged in to Facebook but has not authorized information for your site, an approval message is displayed to the user when your site tries to publish a one-line story. For other story sizes, previews are displayed, which the user can then approve.

- If the user is not logged in, nothing can be published.

Plug-ins that work with Facebook Connect and Open Graph

Facebook has developed many plug-ins that work with Connect and Open Graph programming to make sign in and other user activity seamless. Users who trust the site already do not have to retype login information or can be assured that their login information updates automatically. To learn more about the plug-ins available, check out the Facebook Connect Plugin Directory (https://developers.facebook.com/docs/plugins) to help all developers and bloggers find plug-ins that easily integrate into their sites and blogs. The directory enables users to create, list, and offer or sell their own plug-ins (see Figure 5.15).

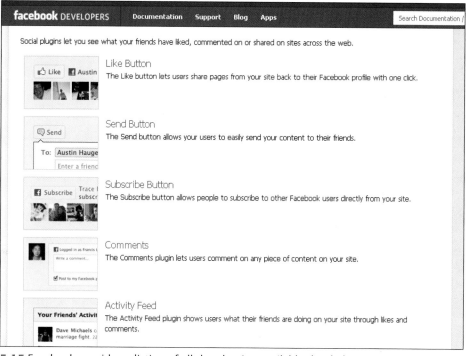

5.15 Facebook provides a listing of all the plug-ins available that help you connect to your website or blog to encourage interaction between the different platforms.

Other integration ideas

Beyond Facebook Connect and Open Graph, there are a few simple touches you can use to create an integrated digital appearance between your website and Facebook.

A meta description

One small coding detail on websites and blogs that increases your visibility is the meta description on a web page. In the HTML code of your website, you can include a description of your website and the particular web page. Speak with your local web developer about how to code meta tags on your website in particular descriptions. The description is visible on a post. The description has always been available to search engines and has been part of an essential step with search engine optimization. Search engines use your description meta tags to give a preview of your website before a user opens the entire site.

If you are not HTML-savvy, do not worry. The description is very easy to spot. In an HTML page, the code for a meta description looks like this:

```
<meta name="description" content="Here's what's happening at my store this week" />
```

You can also view it in a web page's code by clicking on the page source or view code selection in your web browser. To view your meta tags in Internet Explorer version 9, right-click on the website in question and then click View and then Source.

Regardless of how you view the code, you can use the meta description to your advantage. Insert useful words that depict the purpose of the content, particularly if the page has a Like button. Just make sure that you really explain your page in the first sentence or two.

Here is what a page looks like when the Share button is clicked (see Figure 5.16). The description is the same as what is shown in the content=" " segment of the meta description code. This simple step lets people know what to expect from the page.

5.16 Inserting the meta description on your website increases your visibility within Facebook by improving link sharing and enabling you to tailor the link description.

Also consider the images you use on your pages and ensure that they relate to your subject, as any of them can be potentially selected as the thumbnail for your shared content. When someone shares one of your website posts on Facebook, Facebook automatically attempts to include at least one image from the web page. If there is more than one image, Facebook gives the person sharing the page the option of selecting which image to use — or that person can opt to not use any image when sharing the post.

The point is to use everything at your disposal to identify your post, making it interesting enough for people to share. You can also build your social media image by making it clear that the articles you share are helpful for the audience. If the page is an e-commerce site, describe your product with keyword terms that people are potentially using. Finally, appreciate the ease in which this description can be created. If you are already managing search engine optimization, adding a meta description is not too extensive an extra step because it is also a part of an optimization plan from the start.

Facebook plug-ins

Adding Facebook plug-ins to your website can improve the overall look and boost interaction with potential customers. Plug-ins have a specific purpose that may not be revenue generating, but their appearance on a web page can pique interest to encourage others to work with you. Most plug-ins are available via a simple code you add to your page, or a web developer can help you. You can adjust the width (if your widget is to fit into a column) as well as the color and some other details. Here are some of the plug-ins you can try:

- **Facepile.** The Facepile plug-in shows the people who have liked your page or joined your website, providing social proof of activity and interest in your business.

- **Like Box.** The Like Box plug-in can display your latest fan Page posts in a widget clickable on your site. Facebook users who discover your page can like a post without leaving the website. Moreover, the widget displays the names of other Facebook connections who have also liked the page. Site visitors seeing that their friends have liked your page or website have social proof that can entice them to click on the widget and like the page as well. This may also sound as if a visitor would be drawn from the site, but the right placement of a Like Box plug-in can encourage others to take action on your site. The widget can be just as powerful as a better business bureau or membership seal.

- **Comments Box.** The Comments Box is another useful plug-in that enables a user to comment on your site. If a user leaves the Post to Facebook check box selected when she posts a comment, a story appears on her friends' News Feeds indicating that the person has made a comment on your website, which also links back to your site. A Comments Box measures the quantity and quality of comments (how much they are shared, how often, and so on) to surface the highest-quality comments for each user. Comments are ordered to show users the most relevant comments from friends, friends of friends, and the most liked or active discussion threads, while comments marked as spam are hidden from view. This makes the Comments Box a specifically tailored way of displaying social proof to Facebook users who have arrived to your site, haven't "fanned" your page, but have friends and connections who have.

Social media icon

Just as Facebook plug-ins can appear on a web page to pique interest, Facebook icons can appear in blogs and other online digital media to ensure that people come to your Facebook Page. You can use a number of sources for blogs, for example. Here are a few sources:

- **SexyBookmarks.** (http://shareaholic.com/publishers/sharing) This is a WordPress plug-in and a catchall for social media links. The user can select which social media icons appear in an array at the bottom of a post.

- **Wibiya.** (http://wibiya.conduit.com) This one is that mysterious bar that scrolls up from the bottom of a web page view. Offered by Conduit, this application is customizable and allows viewers to click a link to a social media site of the user's choice.

- **Custom buttons.** There are a ton of sites with HTML codes for custom Facebook buttons. Just type the phrase **social media icons** in a search engine, and you find a number of websites where you can copy code for your own site.

Adding these plug-ins should not require any coding and should take only a few minutes to install. The most important aspect is making sure that these are available. With Facebook's popularity, it is essential that these links are easy for readers to see and click.

Website versus Facebook-Only Presence

As Facebook development and offerings increased over the years, there has been some debate among marketers and pundits about whether a Facebook presence in place of a standard website would be best in the long run. Part of the reasoning has been due to the audience Facebook has generated. An eMarketer report in February 2011 titled "Facebook Reaches Majority of U.S. Web Users" indicated that Facebook reached 57 percent of Internet users and nine out of ten users of social media. So many professionals argue that a Facebook-only presence would gain more exposure than any effort committed for a website, such as search engine marketing.

Despite Facebook's enormous audience, maintaining a website as well as a Facebook presence is the best tactic. The most significant reason to maintain a website is the simple fact that you own the website and completely control the content and functionality of that site. With a Facebook Page, you are at the mercy of the Facebook platform and its controls and functionality. A website can provide visual branding for your customers — it can be designed to closely imitate your building, for example. A website can also permit the development of navigation features that may not be developed as easily within Facebook. Moreover, eliminating a website would eliminate many options for integrating your website and Facebook, such as Like buttons and Facepiles, which allow a larger market reach, encourage new visits to your site, and engender trust. Finally, many analytic solutions for Facebook Pages are not as nuanced as those for websites and blogs. The solutions are meant to help you understand interaction with respect to a Facebook Page, but not necessarily clickstream analysis — how people navigate through a website. As a result, you lose the ability to understand how segmented audiences receive certain content as well as the ability to test for improvements that can increase online sales or leads.

Nevertheless, a Facebook Page and a website or blog can complement each other and create an impressive, coherent presence for your business (see Figure 5.17). Moreover, do not assign Facebook to second-rate status by not developing special content and strategies of engagement for it. Remember that Facebook has a gigantic audience reach that spends a considerable amount of time on the social network. Treat a website and Facebook presence with equal importance, respecting and leveraging their differences.

5.17 A cohesive connection between your website, Facebook Page, and blog creates strong marketing of your brand and delivers a coherent impression to visitors.

How a Cake Recipe Website Integrates with Facebook

How are real small businesses using Facebook and their websites to better engage customers?

Vladimir Prelovac, founder and CEO of Prelovac Media, a social media consulting firm in Belgrade, Serbia, analyzes TorteKolaci.com, a Serbian blog offering cake recipes. The following sections take a look at how this website is using Facebook.

Facebook Like button

Using a basic Facebook widget is another way of saying you like something that you find on a site, but with one important difference: your preference will be visible on your profile Page for all your friends to see. The recipe on TorteKolaci.com for ice cube cake has 4,000 likes, a number even sites like Mashable would envy. Almost 4,000 likes on a single recipe. We have a Facebook Like button two times on the Page so you don't miss it (see Figure 5.18).

5.18 Over 4,000 people have viewed and liked this single recipe on TorteKolaci.com.

Facebook comments

Receiving comments on your website or blog is great and there are a variety of easy ways to enable comments (see Figure 5.19). Facebook also has a solution, which enables you to manage comments on your website with Facebook. On his blog, Vladimir has written about TorteKolaci.com changing its comment system so that it is integrated with Facebook. To start using Facebook's comment system in your website, check out its social plug-ins at http://developers.facebook.com/docs/reference/plugins/comments.

Facebook Like option

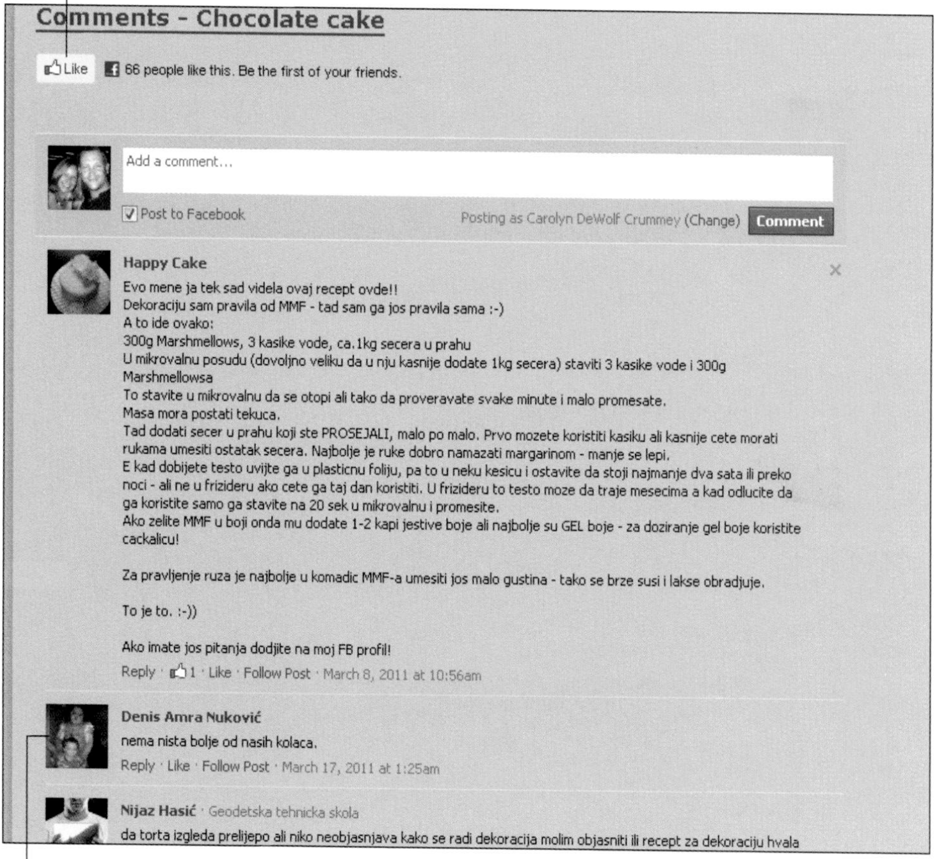

Facebook comments

5.19 By allowing comments to appear on its website from Facebook, TorteKolaci.com saw an instant increase in participation.

"Before the change, we received around 5 to 10 comments daily," Vladimir wrote. "After the change this number jumped up immediately to 20 to 30 comments a day! Main reason seems to be easier accessibility, as now the user can start writing the comment immediately (provided they are already logged into Facebook, which most of them are). Compared to a standard blog comment form where you need to type in your name, e-mail, and website, Facebook comments are much more likely to be used (in our experience around three times more likely)."

An added bonus of Facebook comments is that the user can easily post the comment directly to his or her profile Page. That brings more attention not only to the comment but also to the related Page.

Facebook group

You join groups in the offline world (Sunday school, Boy Scouts, professional associations, chambers of commerce, and so on), and online the world is very similar. You want to join groups of like-minded people, hence the growth of Meetup. With this in mind, the marketers at TorteKolaci created a Facebook group for lovers of sweets. According to Vladimir, the group has more than 9,000 members and is growing every day. Group members engage by sharing their stories, recipes, and photos.

Instead of a default Facebook group widget, Vladimir created his own, which blends into TorteKolaci's site much better (see Figure 5.20).

"I am still not sure whether this has positive or negative impact on new member sign ups (as this kind of test would be hard to set up), but my gut feeling says positive," Vladimir wrote.

 NOTE See Chapter 3 for more information on using groups and an explanation of the differences between Facebook Pages and groups.

Facebook Like   Share

Facepile   Fan Page

5.20 TorteKolaci.com marketers created their own group, or fan Page, button for their website. As you can see, they also do a fabulous job of incorporating other available Facebook plug-ins (such as Facepile) on their website to generate interaction and interest in the site.

| **Timeline** | **Info** | **Photos** | **Notes** |

Creating Facebook Events

Hosting a crowd is one thing, but how should your small business get the word out about events? Well, sure enough, Facebook has a tool for announcing events. Facebook Events lets you organize gatherings with your customers, partners, employees, and other people in your community.

Professional event managers or businesses with a frequent exhibit production schedule can leverage the Facebook Events app. Successful event management requires an understanding of the audience you are trying to attract. There's no better way to manage your message than within Facebook, given that so many of its tools enable you to reach your desired event attendees with ease. This chapter looks at some details specific to the Events app and how to best use it.

Creating an Event in Facebook

So you have a special event planned for your business and now it's time to let everyone know. Facebook is the perfect tool to get the information about an event to your customers and your larger following. The Events app within Facebook allows you to create Events and post them to your business Page. It also enables you to invite individual followers or groups. Who might post an Event on Facebook? Here are some examples:

- A music artist promoting a new album has a launch party
- A writer promoting the latest novel or nonfiction book has a book signing
- A retailer creating an in-store promotion
- A small business owner mentioning an upcoming webinar
- An organization offering an open house mixer
- A nonprofit creating a fundraising project

Events that you post on Facebook appear in a separate box in the views and apps on your business Page and, once created, are public by default. The Events Page displays your upcoming Events, any invitations you have pending, and links to your own Events.

To create an Event using Facebook Events, follow these steps:

1. **Go to your Facebook business Page and click Event, Milestone below your cover photo (see Figure 6.1).**

2. **Click the Event button to go to the Event details box.**

3. **Fill out the Create New Event dialog box.** It is pretty straightforward (see Figure 6.2):

   a. Type the Event name.

   b. Add details about the event.

   c. Add the location.

   d. Select the date and time.

   e. Select or deselect the Show guest list check box and the Only admins can post to the Event wall check box.

6.1 To create an event, click Event, Milestone on your business Page to access the event details screen.

6.2 Add the Event specifics.

When you finish, click Create Event, and you are off to the races. You have created an Event ready for everyone to share. The new Event appears in the Events box under your cover photo on your business Page so that anyone visiting your Page can click to see the details of this Event and all Events you have (see Figure 6.3).

Events box

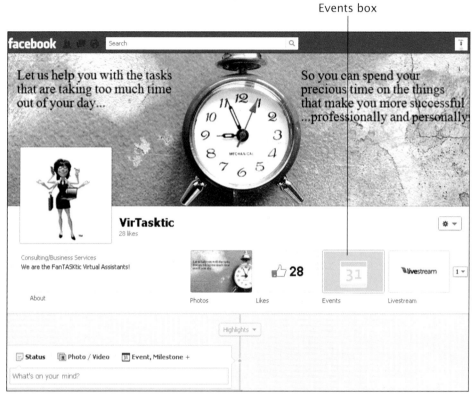

6.3 Your current and past Events appear in the Events box under the cover photo of your Page.

Unlike an Event you create under your personal account, business Page Events are public by default and anyone can join them, therefore there is no invitation list for the Event.

In addition to the basic Event information, you can also add a picture in the Event details to entice more attendees. You can do this by opening the Event and simply hovering your mouse over the large date box on the left until you see the Add Event Photo link. Click that link and select an image to include on the Event posting (see Figure 6.4).

6.4 Add a photo to your Event to make it more appealing to potential guests.

Announcing Your Event

There are several ways that people on Facebook can discover your Event announcement:

- **Sidebar announcement on their home page.** The right column lists a few of the most current upcoming Events. The Event can also appear in a listing on the left column as well.

- **Their News Feed.** When the Event is created, it appears in the News Feed of those who like your business Page.

Events created in a profile Page can be directed to followers as a personal invite. The notification appears in the person's Messages in Facebook or is delivered via personal e-mail (if that person's e-mail notification is on).

When you set up your Event using your business Page, you are required to post your Event on the Timeline and do not have the option of sending invites to individual guests during the setup.

To recap, when the Event is created on a business Page, you can only send updates to the Timeline as a notification. Profile Page setup lets you send personal e-mails to people directly for Event updates. The e-mails typically are more visible to recipients because they are direct.

There are minor notification differences with business Pages and profile Pages that you must keep in mind when starting out on Facebook and planning to promote Events. The difference makes sense: Think of a personal profile as your own home. You may be having a party, but you wouldn't invite the whole world.

Another notable detail is that Events do not permit repeated notifications. This means you have to manually issue the Event notices to get people to know your Event is forthcoming. That can be a little challenging, but you can use social media dashboards to schedule Event notifications automatically.

Creating Livestream Events

Live events have become all the rage online. Increases in computing capability and better video technology have made live video available for virtually everyone. Adding a live stream can be helpful for regularly scheduled programs as well as one-time events such as panel discussions. It shows what people can expect from participating in your event in-person, displaying the immediate interactions of attendees. Organizations of all types have leveraged live streaming. Even some churches have live stream services to help those who cannot attend a regular service. So live streaming can accommodate a number of varied services.

There are a number of applications available to stream events live on Facebook. Some vendors include Ustream, Vpype, Justin.tv, and Livestream. Naturally, each has a variation of features, with free and paid versions available.

Here is an example of how to live stream on Facebook using Livestream:

1. **Go to the Livestream app on Facebook at http://apps.facebook.com/ livestream.**
2. **Click Get Started (see Figure 6.5).**

6.5 Click Get Started on the Livestream app Page to begin installing to your Facebook Page.

3. **Click Allow to allow the app to access your Facebook Page (see Figure 6.6).**

 NOTE Livestream also offers custom design services for Facebook apps. For more information or for pricing inquiries, go to http://new.livestream.com/broadcast-live/design-custom-facebook-apps.

Request for Permission

Livestream is requesting permission to do the following:

Access my basic information
Includes name, profile picture, gender, networks, user ID, list of friends, and any other information I've made public

Manage my pages
Livestream may login as any of my 2 Pages, including:

- VirTasktic
- VirTasktic

Post to Facebook as me
Livestream may post status messages, notes, photos, and videos on my behalf.

Access my data any time
Livestream may access my data when I'm not using the application.

By proceeding, you agree to Livestream's Terms of Service and Privacy Policy · Report App

Logged in as Carolyn DeWolf Crummey · Log Out   Allow   Don't Allow

6.6 As with most apps, you have to allow the application to access your Page information.

4. **Click the Add Page Tab button beside the Page where you want the Livestream app to appear (see Figure 6.7).**

5. **Click Add Livestream.**

6. **Click the Livestream link on the left side of your Facebook Page (see Figure 6.8).**

facebook 🙎 💬 🌐 | Search 🔍

▲livestream for Facebook

| ⦿ Broadcast Now | Help & Services |

Add a Livestream tab to any of your Facebook pages!   Hide this message

Simply click the "Add Page Tab" button. You will be able to choose a channel (or create a new one) on the page tab once it's created. Want to start a new Facebook page? Click here.

🗆 **Pages with Livestream**

| (r·TASK·tic VirTasktic | ⚠ |
| Installed but channel not set | |

🗅 **Pages without Livestream**

| 📍 | VirTasktic | ? | äh Massage Bar |
| | ♦ Add Page Tab | | ♦ Add Page Tab |

Help and Services   ▲livestream

                                        👤⦿ Chat (Offline)

6.7 The application asks you to choose which Page you want to add the application to.

7. **Click Start New Channel.**

8. **Open a new Livestream account and click Signup (see Figure 6.9).**

9. **Install the Livestream software on your PC or Mac.**

10. **Connect your video camera.**

11. **Review your video camera instructions for details on how your video camera can connect to your PC and transmit video signal via USB or other connectivity.** Once your camera is properly transmitting, you see what the camera is capturing on your computer screen in the Livestream. This sounds complicated, but I've taught many nontechnical people to do this many times.

You're now ready to start streaming your first live event on Facebook.

139

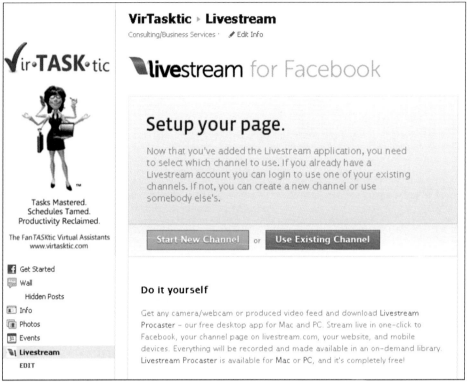

6.8 Once the app is installed, you can click the link box in the views and apps section of your Page to access Livestream.

Livestream is widely used in Facebook, and offers a number of services that permit you to create broadcasts with full capability ranging from simple broadcast to a network. Here are a few other live streaming options:

- **Vpype.** (http://vpype.com) Founded in 2009, Vpype is specifically designed for Facebook. It provides an application for greeting your connections as well as other versions that relate to specific types of events.

- **Ustream.** (www.ustream.tv/facebook) Ustream also has similar features. It permits the display of past performances as well as the main event front and center.

- **Justin.tv.** (www.facebook.com/Justintv) Justin.tv organizes streams around searchable topics such as sports, news, and entertainment.

Signup link

✔ir•TASK•tic

Tasks Mastered.
Schedules Tamed.
Productivity Reclaimed.

The FanTASKtic Virtual Assistants
www.virtasktic.com

🄵 Get Started
🖳 Wall
   Hidden Posts
🔲 Info
📷 Photos
📅 Events
📺 **Livestream**
   EDIT

About   ✎ Edit
We are the FanTASKtic Virtual
Assistants!

Channel Settings   ✖ Cancel

◉ **My channel**   Don't have a Livestream account? Signup

Login with your Livestream account
If you don't have an account you can create a new one, or show an existing
channel without the need to login. Please note, to broadcast using Livestream
Procaster (our free desktop broadcasting app for Mac and PC) you will need a
Livestream login.

Username: [   ]

Password: [   ]

[Login]   Forgot your password? Click here

○ **Other channel**   No Livestream account required
   livestream.com/ [   ]

   ☐ Show Chat   ☐ Show Video Library
   [Select Channel]

6.9 Once you set up a Livestream account, you begin to stream live events through your Page.

Live events are not easy, but successful ones can build your brand in a big way. Beyond live streaming of events, there are other online networks and communities that can complement Facebook. Some of these services are focused on a particular audience, such as ReverbNation, for example. It has sharing features specific for the needs of music artists and professionals. You can combine your use of these specialty platforms with Facebook for more efficient notification of offers and events.

Econsultancy, an information site and community for digital marketing and e-commerce professionals, posted a number of great tips for conducting a live event on its blog (http://econsultancy.com/us/blog). Here are some of those tips:

- Pick a hashtag for people to tweet if they want to share details in Twitter. Have the hashtag visible at the app window or on points on-screen.

- Use some of the best comments from the live event to generate online content.

- Respond to comments quickly — the positive comments as well as the negative comments.

- Partner with other organizations that sponsor the event to promote the live stream. Doing so can help spread the word to a large audience.

- If you have employees, ask them to share the live streaming event on their profiles as well as updates leading to the event.

- Try to keep the conversation on topic. It's great to allow spontaneity when appropriate, but eliminate spam-like topics when the chatter seems to eat up time.

- Have an emergency plan for disruptors if your event addresses a controversial topic.

- Let people know if the event is being recorded. Tell them when you expect to post the program (usually a few days after the live event is acceptable) as well as where viewers can see the post.

Promoting Your Event

Once your event details are submitted and your notification is sent, you must decide the degree of promotion you want to conduct. Sending a reminder or two is okay for a small event where you are looking for an intimate gathering of contacts. However, for business, more than likely you should have an active effort that builds up to the event.

Keep Facebook general rules and acceptable behavior in mind. For example, like posting repeated statuses on a Timeline, sending repeated updates is not a great idea. Let your community know about the event, but do so without a heavy-handed sales approach. A repeated message is ignored on most social media channels, but it is especially a bother on Facebook. Who wants a Facebook Timeline full of "Come to my play"? Many organizations forget this in social media without stepping back and realizing that people decide what they want to pay attention to. To prevent spamming, send event reminders periodically. Use social media dashboards to schedule the static reminders: You can make periodic spur-of-the-moment I-am-excited-for-XYZ-event posts to stir things up. A little spontaneity is acceptable and natural.

A second tip is to develop teaser content for the event. Photos showing event preparation or simple "Look what is coming soon" posts are great ways to share the excitement of your event. Posting teasers that lead up to the event lets people understand your offering without spamming everyone's profiles. You can also post photos from past events to show proof of past success to newcomers.

Remember that not everyone sees your update the instant you share it. It's good practice to repost your posts later in the day or even later in the week. I post many of my posts a week later, sometimes with a different angle or spin.

Aside from sharing your events on your website or blog, you can participate in communities and talk to members who potentially share an interest in your event theme. Keep in mind the spam rule in any community — do not butt in with your "grand" announcement. Instead, try to participate in communities prior to the event; either do it yourself or assign an employee. Even better, make a contribution to community needs, such as the question-and-answer panels. Your community effort will help make your promotions softer instead of intrusive hard sells.

For promoting within Facebook, all the standard tools can be applied (such as Facebook ads and Sponsored Stories). You should use tools that will make your event discoverable by your intended audience and augment other marketing efforts. For example, you can set Facebook ads for a region in which you cannot penetrate due to limited budget or limited resources.

As in the real world, give yourself ample time for your event to catch on. Instant response is not always the case when posting online — people discover your announcement when they do. So make sure you have enough buildup to the day of the event.

Finally, following up on an event is a sign of thoughtfulness. Sending follow-up material can encourage someone to attend future events. Particularly in the cases of missed attendance, a "Sorry you couldn't make it" note helps. Links to webinar recaps or video replays can be shared by others and provide a way to see the missed event. Even better, you can ask people to share their thoughts about the event recaps on your Facebook business Page or the Event Page, itself.

Using Other Event Apps

There are other apps that permit posting event announcements to your Facebook Page. Eventbrite, for example, connects your events to Facebook (see Figure 6.10). Events created in Eventbrite are automatically added to the Facebook Events app, permitting easy integration of event awareness among followers. Go to www.eventbrite.com/t/facebook-connect-eventbrite for more information. Although the ability to sell event tickets cannot be natively integrated into the Facebook Event Page, Mashable notes that "Eventbrite will include a link to your event's ticketing Page in the event description and a link to 'Order Tickets' in the News Feed insertion about your event."

Another popular community site, Meetup, permits announcements of events created on its site on Facebook profiles. This permits a Meetup user to share with others who are on Facebook as well as on Meetup. As a member of a Meetup, you can determine who also uses Facebook and notify them of your event.

Probably the nicest feature of Facebook is being able to integrate the best of other sites into the notification system of the world's most active community. No matter what your event, you'll find that consistent use of the aforementioned tips will bring great success to your event.

6.10 Eventbrite allows you to post your event directly to your Facebook Page and links back to the Event Page for those who want to purchase tickets.

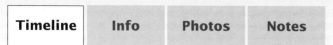

chapter 7

Timeline | Info | Photos | Notes

Using Facebook to Generate Local Store Foot Traffic

There are about 30 million small businesses in the United States with physical locations that depend on walk-in foot traffic. While foot traffic and face-to-face customer service are essential for repeat business, online engagement with those customers helps bring them back. Local shoppers enjoy telling friends about the Check-in Deals they find. Facebook Places and Check-in Deals list local businesses and their current promotions, empowering business owners to drive traffic to their locations. Individuals can share that they are at your location along with the Check-in Deals you are offering. These services are examined in detail in this chapter.

Your Local Business and Facebook

The first few chapters of this book cover the marketing reach you can obtain by using Facebook for your small business. As I've mentioned, Facebook has created numerous applications that help drive people back to your website or e-commerce site. But Facebook is not limited to the Internet and a virtual association to your business. Facebook has also developed applications that help drive foot traffic to your physical business location. As much as I've stressed the importance of having a Facebook Page for your business and incorporating applications into your website, creating links to your physical business location is just as essential, and an amazing and economical way to market your business.

Using Facebook Places as a customer

If you have a business with a physical location, Facebook Places can be an amazing tool for you. Places is a check-in program that lets Facebook users indicate where they are so that their followers (or just friends) can join them at the location if they wish. Facebook Places is designed specifically for physical locations to connect with people using mobile devices. A Facebook Places user checks in to a place or organization that has established its Places presence in Facebook via a Place Page. Friends of the user can see the Places notification and can choose to join the user at the location or allow the notification to be a discovery of a new place to visit later (see Figure 7.1).

7.1 Each time you check in at a location, your activity appears in your News Feed for all your friends to see along with the friends of anyone you tag with you.

This Check-In feature enables you to do the following:

- Check in to a location and post an update that appears on the Place Page, your friends' News Feeds, and your Timeline.
- Tag the friends you are with so they can be part of the update.
- Browse status updates of friends checked in nearby.
- After checking in, tap the Here Now button on the application to see who else is checked in where you are.

Finally, Facebook Places enables you to find local Check-in Deals:

- Use Facebook Places on your mobile device to find special offers everywhere. Once you check in to a location on your device, any special Check-in Deals that are offered appear under your Check-in status and are represented with the Check-in Deal logo ( ).
- Save at your favorite retailers, eateries, and entertainment venues.
- Check in to claim a Check-in Deal and let friends know about it.

You can use any supported mobile device to check in on Facebook and let your friends know where you are. Follow these steps:

1. **When you access your mobile Facebook application, tap the ☰ icon.**
2. **Tap Nearby (see Figure 7.2).**
3. **Choose your location from the list that appears, or tap More Nearby Places to search for your location (see Figure 7.3).**

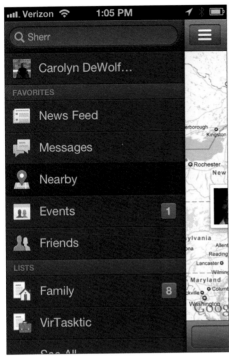

7.2 Tap Nearby to find a list of locations around you and select the one where you are.

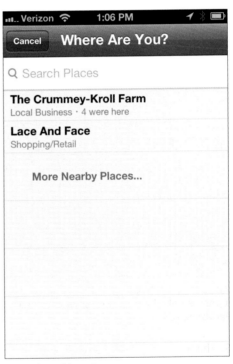

7.3 A list of locations near you appears or you can manually enter your location if it has not already been added.

4. **You can choose to write a post about what you are doing, add friends you are with, or add a picture of the location and then tap Post (see Figure 7.4).**

It's that simple. Now your friends can see not only what you are doing but also where you are. When you post you can also decide who can see your location — friends, the public, or any other combination.

7.4 Once you choose your location, you can add who you are with, add pictures, and create a post, all of which appear on your Timeline and the Timeline of the location (if it has a Facebook Page).

So this is the end user, or customer, side of Facebook Places. What does this mean for your business? The Facebook Places application makes it easier to extend your marketing reach for almost no cost. Additionally, it validates your business by allowing users and their activity to be a testimonial of your business, products, and services.

Moreover, Places can provide a vital means for leveraging your interaction with people through their mobile devices because they have to come to your business to redeem a Check-in Deal. While Facebook Places is fun and engaging for individuals — your potential customers — it's a serious business tool and local (in-person) engagement tool.

Establishing a Facebook Place Page for your business

Businesses are quickly discovering the benefit of Facebook Places. Woods Coffee, a 100-employee coffee shop chain based in Whatcom County, Washington, uses Facebook Place extensively. Jessica Stuart, the social media director for the 10-shop local chain, said in a case study that she uses the business's Place as "a place for our customers to get the current info on what's new, what's happening, and lately to get their questions answered" (see Figure 7.5).

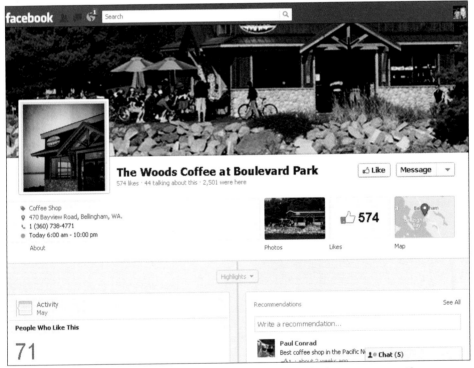

7.5 Woods Coffee does an excellent job of using its Facebook Place Page to notify customers of current happenings and Check-in Deals.

You can use Facebook Places to simply encourage users to check in on their mobile devices when they visit your business. This check-in is shared with their friends, exposing your local business to the friends of any user who checks in to your business.

Setting up a Place Page

The setup begins by locating your business or organization through the Facebook application on a mobile device. You must physically be at your place of business to do this, as Facebook uses your current location to search for nearby businesses. Tap Nearby on the application and then tap Check In. Search for the name of your business or organization in the Facebook search box. If your business or organization name does not appear in the results, then you can create the Page by typing your name and tapping Add. You can then enter an optional description of the business (see Figure 7.6). Once that is done, tap the Add button in the upper right again and you can then check in to the location that you have created.

 NOTE You must be at the location of your business when checking in to ensure that the proper location is saved in Facebook.

7.6 If your business does not appear in the search when you check in at your location, you can simply add it and a brief description so that it appears on Facebook.

Once the Place Page is created, the next step is to claim the Page, which you must do directly from Facebook (not on a mobile device). You will find a post in your News Feed that announces that you checked in to your business location (see Figure 7.7). Click the name of your business in that post to go to the created Page. Click on the utilities box in the upper-right corner of the Page to access the drop-down list. Click the Is this your business? link. A Claim Your Business pop-up menu appears where you can select a check box that verifies that you are the representative of the Page (see Figure 7.8). Select the check box and click Continue to advance to Verify Page Info where you can provide the business name, address, phone number, website, and additional information (see Figure 7.9). In order to claim the Page, you have to either verify through an e-mail address or documentation to complete the process.

7.7 Once you check in to your location from your mobile device, you find a notification with the business name in your News Feed that you can click to connect to.

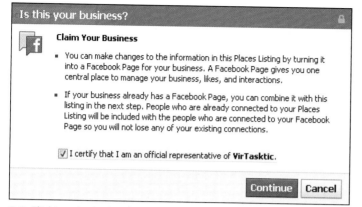

Is this your business?

Claim Your Business

- You can make changes to the information in this Places Listing by turning it into a Facebook Page for your business. A Facebook Page gives you one central place to manage your business, likes, and interactions.

- If your business already has a Facebook Page, you can combine it with this listing in the next step. People who are already connected to your Places Listing will be included with the people who are connected to your Facebook Page so you will not lose any of your existing connections.

☑ I certify that I am an official representative of **VirTasktic**.

[Continue] [Cancel]

7.8 Clicking the Is this your business? link allows you to claim your business Page and verify that you are the owner.

Business Information

Please provide additional information about your business:

Official name of business: [VirTasktic]

Street address: [   ]

City/State: [   ]

Zip Code: [   ]

Phone number (if available): [   ]

Website (if available): [   ]

[Claim] [Cancel]

7.9 After you claim the Page, you can fill in all the details of your business so that future visitors can find you.

Adding details to your Place Page

Once you claim your Page, you can begin setting up the details. To have your local business listed in Facebook Places, you must be listed in the Local Business or Place category. This ensures that local visitors can indicate they are at your location. Setting up a Facebook Place Page requires steps similar to arranging a Facebook business Page. If needed, refer to Chapter 2 for more information on setting up your Facebook business Page.

To set up a Place Page, begin at the Create a Page site at www.facebook.com/pages/create.php and choose the Local Business or Place category.

A Place Page works similar to a personal or business Page, so a number of the tools and strategies that work on a Page are also applicable in this instance. The first step is building a Timeline, a space where all posts from admins and fans can post. The Timeline looks like any other profile T showing the latest posts, but it incorporates a significant difference. The Timeline permits a Places-participating business to show posts from everyone in a variety of settings.

You might find that you have a Facebook Page and a Facebook place. Instead of having two Facebook destinations, having one is best so that you can focus on engaging on Facebook in one place. When you create your Facebook place, Facebook might detect that you have a similar Facebook Page. You will have the option to merge an existing Page to your new Facebook place.

To set the Timeline setting to this level of interaction, click Edit Page and go to the Manage Permissions section to adjust who can post on your Timeline and set the moderation filters.

Just as with your business Page, the Like button is how users connect to your Place. When a person clicks Like, a News Feed story is shared with his or her friends (for example, Sabrina likes your Page).

The navigation links to your Pages and applications appears below your cover photo. The prepopulated links may vary depending on your Place category. Click Edit to move and delete links.

Your Place Page should contain a cover photo, just like your business Page. The process of updating is exactly the same as with your business or personal Page. Remember, the cover photo is a great place to showcase your brand and your products or services. Get creative! It's a large piece of real estate that should be used to its fullest potential. You may want to use photos of people in your business or organization in action, from a waitress serving a meal to employees at a nonprofit using newly gained donations to make a difference in a community. Your picture should reflect what customers who come to your business or organization can expect.

I encourage you to use some of the tools covered in earlier chapters such as polls, photos, and links related to your products and services on your Place's Wall. And don't forget to regularly publish updates to your Wall as well as photos and videos. The content will appear on the Wall and in the News Feeds of people who like your Place, which keeps you constantly in front of your market. Moreover, if the media is interesting, people will share the posts with their friends, increasing the circle of awareness the posts generate. For example, if you post photos that include people who have liked your Place Page, they will likely be tagged by those same people. Their tags will appear in their feeds, drawing their friends and followers to look at the photos and consequently your Place Page. Those friends and followers may have decided to like your Place as well. This is the digital equivalent of word of mouth. These new followers may later come to your business. Thus, posting a photo is an initial step for branding.

Here are some tips for improving your Place Page:

- The number of people who like your Place appears under your cover photo.

- Likes shows a list of other Pages that your Place is affiliated with or interested in. To feature a Page you like, click the Page's Like button when you are using Facebook as your Place. Then click Edit Page option on your own Page and select the Page in the Featured section.

- You can feature Page Administrators and link to their personal profiles from your Place. To feature a Page administrator, click Edit Page (top right of the Page) and select Admin in the Featured section.

- Be sure to answer questions, address concerns, and acknowledge when people take the time to post on your Place's Wall.

You may feel stuck creating content updates for your Place, but there are plenty of ways to do it. Restaurants, for example, can showcase food, educate customers about the food they serve, share the press they receive, and show off their best plates. Encouraging customer comments and responding immediately to customer requests shows that you care about your relationships. Moreover, employees with a mobile app can respond on the go. Jessica Stuart of Woods Coffee mentions in a case study that the app on her mobile phone is a lifesaver. "I have found it easy updating from my iPhone wherever I am. I can update our status, reply to a Wall post, and upload a mobile picture."

The ultimate key to creating quality Place Page content is to be informative, interesting, and consistent in maintaining your offline and online image (see Figure 7.10).

7.10 Margaritas Mexican Restaurant does a great job of showcasing its food, events, and customer comments on its Facebook Place Page.

Using Facebook Check-in Deals

So, you've learned about a great way to connect people to your physical location, which should get people in the door and help generate additional revenue, but there's more! Another way to generate actual revenue from Facebook Places is to provide local Check-in Deals and incentives to your customers based on a variety of options related to their check-in status. Keep in mind that the Check-in Deals feature is in limited beta, so for the time being not all Places will be able to create Check-in Deals.

Check-in Deals are meant to augment your Place presence and are a great way to build your business. They increase customer loyalty with your most interested audience, spread the word about your business, and help attract new customers. To redeem a Check-in Deal, customers click Get Offer in the headline of the offer and send the offer to the e-mail address associated with their main Facebook account. Your customer then shows the e-mail to you (or your staff) to redeem the offer.

There are four types of Check-in Deals that you can create, each designed to reach different business objectives:

- **Individual.** This is a one-time Check-in Deal that you can offer to both new and existing customers. This is a great way to launch a new product, get rid of excess inventory, or just get more people into your store (see Figure 7.11).

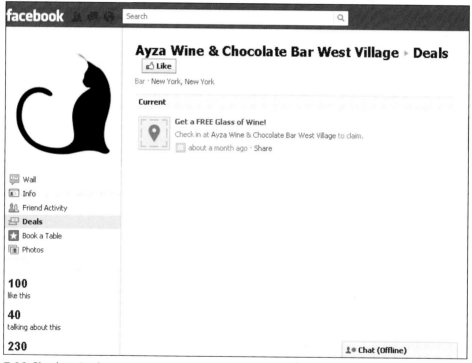

7.11 Check-in Deals appear on the Facebook mobile application to anyone searching in your area. They are a great way to encourage foot traffic to your location.

- **Loyalty.** This is a Check-in Deal to reward your loyal customers. This Check-in Deal is given after your customer reaches a set amount of check-ins at your location — you choose the amount.

- **Friend.** Because people usually shop in groups, the Friend Check-in Deal is a great option. You can offer discounts to groups of up to eight people when they check in together. This Check-in Deal gets you even more exposure because in order to claim it, the entire group needs to check in to your Place.

- **Charity.** This Check-in Deal is a great way to show your customers that you care about your community and different causes and encourage them to come to your business. The Charity Check-in Deal makes a donation of an amount you choose to a charity of your choice whenever someone claims the Check-in Deal (see Figure 7.12).

Starbucks ▸ Deals 🔲 Like
Local Business

Deal

We'll donate $1 to help protect forest land

How to Claim   Check in at Starbucks to claim donation.

Availability   Over 100 remaining

Ends   Tuesday, November 30, 2010 at 4:30pm (Pacific Time)

on Wednesday · Share · Report

▫ Profile
👤 Friend Activity
⬜ **Deals**

32 check-ins

1 person likes this

🚩 **Share**

The Value of Facebook Deals: Loyalty, Awareness & Foot Traffic

Loyalty

7.12 Charity Check-in Deals are another great way to generate foot traffic and support a local cause.

To set up a Check-in Deal, click Edit Page on your business's Place Page and choose Deals from the links in the left column (see Figure 7.13).

facebook

VirTasktic

Your Settings
Manage Permissions
Basic Information
Profile Picture
Featured
Resources
Manage Admins
Apps
Mobile
Insights
Help
Deals

Page Visibility:	☐ Unpublish page (only admins can see this page) What is this?
Country Restrictions:	Type a country... What is this?
	◉ Only show this page to viewers in these countries
	○ Hide this page from viewers in these countries
Age Restrictions:	Anyone (13+) ▾ What is this?
Wall Tab Shows:	Only Posts by Page ▾ [?] ☑ Expand comments on stories
Default Landing Tab:	Wall ▾
Posting Ability:	☑ People can write or post content on the wall
	☐ People can add photos and videos
	☐ People can add tags to photos by VirTasktic
Moderation Blocklist:	Comma separated list of terms to block... [?]
Profanity Blocklist:	None ▾ [?]

👤● Chat (Offline)

Deals

7.13 From the edit page you choose Deals from the links menu in the left column to create a Check-in Deal.

The remaining steps are easy (see Figure 7.14):

1. **Choose your Check-in Deal type from one of the four types.**

2. **Define your offer by summarizing the details in the Deal Summary text box and how to claim the Check-in Deal in the How to Claim text box.**

3. **Specify run dates and restrictions and then click Save.**

NOTE   Always create your Check-in Deals at least 48 hours in advance, as all Check-in Deals are subject to review by Facebook. It is also recommended that you run each Check-in Deal for a minimum of a week to allow users the opportunity to take advantage of the offer.

Choose a type of deal:

Individual Deal
Reward individual customers when they check in at your business. Best for simple discounts or gifts with purchase.

Friend Deal
Reward groups of customers when they check in together. Help spread the word about your business more rapidly.

Loyalty Deal
Reward customers for visiting your business a certain number of times, similar to a traditional punch card.

Charity Deal
Pledge to donate to a charity of your choice when customers check in at your business. A win-win for everyone!

50% off any dinner special (Limit 1 per customer)
Check in to claim

Customer view after check-in

50% off any dinner special (Limit 1 per customer)

Present this screen to cashier

Expires in 3 hours · 1 / 100

Define your offer:

Deal Summary: 50% off any dinner special (Limit 1 per customer)
Maximum 50 characters.

How to Claim: Present this screen to cashier
Maximum 100 characters.

Add details and restrictions:

Starting: 2/5/2012   5:00 pm

Ending: 2/12/2012   5:00 pm

Max Redemptions: ⦿ 100
○ Unlimited

Repeat Claims: ⦿ Claimable once every 24 hours per user

💬 Chat (Offline)

7.14 The steps to creating a Check-in Deal are quick and simple.

Using Facebook Places and Check-in Deals for your local marketing

Thanks to the explosion of the Internet, local retailers and local service providers can be quickly and easily connected to their customers. With the added use of smartphones, customers have instant access to the local establishments they want to buy from.

Facebook Places and Check-in Deals lets you boost your local marketing and attract customers right to your door step — day after day. Your customers have lots of choices. The incentives you can offer through Facebook Check-in Deals give them a reason to come back.

Getting customers

Just about every one of your customers carries a smartphone everywhere, and many of them use Check-in Deals. Using Facebook Check-in Deals, you are able to actively connect with them by showing them Check-in Deals at your location if they are signed in to Facebook and set up to be notified of Check-in Deals based on their cell phones' GPS settings.

Spreading the word

The other nice thing about local marketing with Facebook is that when customers check in to your place or redeem a Check-in Deal, they in turn inform their friends through Facebook. Local marketing using Facebook is not only about the actual customers who visit your store and buy from you; it's also about referral marketing, or word-of-mouth marketing, or viral marketing!

Building loyalty

Getting one customer to buy from you is relatively easy. But getting customers to buy from you over and over is much more difficult. Why do you think airlines use frequent-flyer miles? To entice passengers to fly with them over and over again. Local marketing using Facebook Check-in Deals and Check-ins is establishing your own frequent-flyer program on a very local level.

Local Check-in Deal Best Practices

Creating local Check-in Deals, like any advertising, is something you should do with strategic thought and not on a whim. You can use any of the Check-in Deal types to best attract customers and match up to your intended marketing campaign. For example, a loyalty Check-in Deal can implicitly explain to your customers that they are truly VIPs because of their commitment to your business or professional services. A charity Check-in Deal would be a great way to establish your brand and exposure in a neighborhood community.

You can summarize the Check-in Deal in the Deal Summary text box when you create your Check-in Deal. Your description should be enticing but not overdone with a hard sale. Some businesses apply old-school buy-now language in ads. Although you want a customer's attention, moderate the language so that it entices — remember, in social media, people prefer to be engaged, not dictated to.

You can make individual Check-in Deals very personal by creating a summary that highlights the benefit the person receives in the Check-in Deal. For example, a first-time Check-in Deal does not require a heavy handed hard sell in the Check-in Deal description — just ask someone to give it a try. Remember to be direct but not overwhelming.

Here are some other best practices to consider when issuing Check-in Deals for your customers:

- **Offer your customers a lot of value.** Customers take advantage of Check-in Deals when they are enticing and appealing.

- **Write simple copy.** Don't be too complex. Make it simple to understand (see Figure 7.15). You don't want customers spending all day figuring out what your Check-in Deal means. Instead you want them buying from you.

Yvonne Chen claimed a deal at █ SliderBarCafe with Evan Sharp and 3 other people.

20% off any order
24 remaining · 2 days left
Check in here to get this deal.

about an hour ago · Comment · Like

7.15 This Check-in Deal is clear and concise so users know exactly what they are getting and are enticed by the great value.

Is Your Business Ready for Your Check-in Deal?

So you've spent a lot of blood, sweat, and tears (or just some time and money) to create your first Check-in Deal. You come around the block on Tuesday morning (the day of the Check-in Deal) and realize you have lines out the door, frustrated customers, and frustrated staff. What went wrong?

Check out the following tips to ensure you're prepared for the day of the Check-in Deal.

Be proactive

Do a dry run of your Check-in Deal and Check-in to ensure it runs smoothly and that your staff knows how to handle a variety of situations that might come up. You can't anticipate every situation, but you can help your staff plan scenarios. For example, someone who heard about the Check-in Deal but might not have the Check-in Deal to show on her phone. What will you do?

Build your Facebook Place or Page content

Check-in Deals are great, but they're better when you have great content on your Facebook Page to give the customer all the information he needs to take advantage of the Check-in Deal. This information includes business hours, photos, address, and more.

Put yourself in your customers' shoes

Before you market your Check-in Deal, familiarize your staff with mobile phones and Facebook if they are not familiar with these tools and services. Many of your customers might not be familiar with new technology, and your staff's help will be great customer service.

Staff appropriately

Anticipate the customer demand for your Check-in Deal. If you have a well-trafficked store on normal days you can bet that you'll have even more traffic with your Check-in Deal. Make sure you have enough staff (even temporary help) to staff your store.

 NOTE If you have hundreds of store locations, inquire with your account manager and he or she may be able to help you run Check-in Deals more widely. If you have just a few store locations, create each Check-in Deal individually on each store location's Facebook Place. To contact a Facebook account manager, visit www.facebook.com/business/contact.php.

Promoting Your Check-in Campaign

You can promote Check-in Deals in a number of ways. For example, you can share Check-in Deals in your other social media accounts such as Twitter and LinkedIn or on your business's blog posts. Check-in Deals can also be promoted in a Facebook ad if you want to bring awareness within a short period. Using a combination of channels will help spread awareness of the Check-in Deal beyond your initial cadre of customers.

Most advantageously, Facebook makes it possible for potential customers who are nearby to discover the Check-in Deal. Facebook users who use their mobile phone app regularly can opt in to be notified of offers in a neighborhood where they regularly spend time. This means your Check-in Deal will appear if their neighborhood happens to be yours! The Check-in Deal notification arrives in the form of a text message to their phones. If the Check-in Deal piques their interest, customers will come to your business. This makes a Check-in Deal a great new customer acquisition tool, particularly for retail franchises, shops, and restaurants that have a considerable amount of neighborhood foot traffic.

Make sure your store staff is aware of Check-in Deals. Doing so creates a consistent customer service experience by ensuring new customers receive the Check-in Deal they arrived for. Nothing is more annoying for a customer than expecting a Check-in Deal that no one in your business knows about. The experience comes across as a bait-and-switch and results in a lost customer opportunity.

If your Check-in Deal is for a product with a lot of features, such as a mountain bike or a computer, be sure that your employees are knowledgeable about the product. Similar to expecting employees to be knowledgeable about the Check-in Deal, customers want employees to know about the product being sold. If your business offers Check-in Deals regularly, call a short awareness meeting to make sure employees know what is potentially expected. Reviewing the offered Check-in Deals can help prevent employees from going into autopilot and instead provide the initial experiences that lead to long-term customers.

Quote, Unquote: Building Customer Loyalty

"As hard as it is to win a customer's loyalty...you can also lose that customer in a heartbeat if you and your employees ever turn on your autopilot."

— Chris Zane, founder of bicycle retailer Zane Cycles, in his book *Reinventing the Wheel: The Science of Creating Lifetime Customers* (2011)

Using Insights to Understand Your Campaign

After you launch a check-in campaign, you can use Facebook Insights to understand how well a campaign is increasing engagement on your Page. This analysis can be helpful if your business objective for operating a Page is to increase awareness of your services and products or to attract people to a special event at your organization.

To view the results in Facebook Insights, click Insights on the left side of your Page to learn who your audience is and how people interact with your Place Page. Facebook Insights can help measure your engagement on the Place Page. It does so by displaying demographic and geographic information on the people connected to your Page. If you are the administrator of several Place Pages, you can switch between each to understand the engagement metrics.

To learn more about specific features of Facebook Insights, read Chapter 4.

Using Facebook Offers

Facebook Check-in Deals are a great way for local customers to visit your business's retail location. Facebook Offers are similar to Facebook Check-in Deals, except you don't have to check in — you get the offer online, like a digital coupon.

Say you're a law firm and it's tax season. You might want to have a Facebook Offer for procrastinating tax filers that offers 50 percent off your rush tax service. Anyone visiting your Facebook Page can claim this offer, bring it to you, and get 50 percent off your rush tax service.

Offers are a great way to delight visitors on your Facebook Page and encourage them to come to your retail location to redeem. Businesses with franchise locations or national chains might want to leverage Facebook Offers to drive traffic from the mouse to the street.

Like just about everything on Facebook, creating Facebook Offers is not hard to do:

1. **From the Sharing tool on your Facebook Page, right next to where you can update your status, click Offer, Event+.**

2. **Create a compelling headline, as you would with any offer.**

3. **Select how many people can claim this offer.** Two? Twenty-seven?

4. **Decide when this offer should expire.**

5. **Continue through the remaining few options and selections.**

 NOTE As of this writing, Facebook Offers is not available on all Pages. It's in a limited rollout. But I expect that by the time this book is published it will be more widely available.

Your offer is now online for the world to see — especially prospective customers or current customers.

If you want to increase the visibility of your Facebook Offer, consider promoting it through an advertisement or a Sponsored Story.

While it's very easy to create a Facebook Offer, it takes a bit more work to make an offer successful. Here are some things you can do:

- **Give meaningful discounts.** If you're taking the time to make a Facebook Offer, don't make it for 1 percent off or an offer that people can easily get somewhere else. Make it big enough so people care and take the time to take advantage of it. Facebook suggests that 20 percent off is a good starting point, or even buy one, get one free.

- **Use a great image.** Photos are a great way to further engage people to use your offer. Your photo should be clear (not grainy or out of focus) and show how people are using your product. People like seeing your product in action.

- **Don't get fancy with your text.** When making an offer, be clear and to the point. Make sure your headline clearly states the offer right from the beginning.

- **Train your staff.** It's critical that you prepare your staff for the offers that people will bring in to your location. Make sure your staff is aware of the offer and is ready to handle increased traffic as a result.

It's easy for customers to claim an offer: They just click Get Offer below the offer's headline when they see the Offer on your Facebook Page. The offer is then sent to the primary e-mail address associated with the customer's Facebook account. Pretty simple.

 Customers can also claim offers from a mobile device. They can tap Get Offer to have the discount sent to the primary e-mail address associated with their Facebook account.

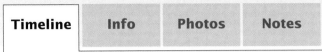

chapter 8

Timeline | Info | Photos | Notes

Catching Media Attention Using Facebook

Public relations professionals have used press releases, close relationships with journalists, and creativity to get "ink" (digital or otherwise) for years. Usually there is the client, the media expert, and the journalist who covers the media expert's client. With the rise of social media, the opportunities (and challenges) for media professionals have increased. Corporate executives have their own Facebook accounts. Journalists can directly engage with companies and their executives on social media networks such as Facebook.

This chapter gives some insight into how Facebook can be used as a powerful tool for getting the attention of journalists so that they cover your brand, product, or service.

Conducting Audience Research

Sarah Skerik, PR Newswire's vice president of social media, is a public relations and social media guru. In an August 2011 blog post, she gives the basics on using Facebook to get more media attention. This section and following sections (through the "Good old-fashioned promotion" section) are written by Sarah and review the key factors that she outlines in PR Newswire's blog to help you understand how to effectively use Facebook to gain media attention.

I'm in the camp that agrees Facebook has a place in public relations strategies. However, the charge to "get it out on Facebook" isn't a tactic I'd recommend. Before one starts communicating via Facebook, it's important to think first about who your audience is. Chances are pretty good that a large chunk of them are on Facebook. But why are they there and how do they use Facebook? Do they tend to be eager and rampant networkers or are they more focused on friends and family? Are they active in groups? Are they enthusiastic game players? A little research into who your audience is will help you develop more messages and strategies.

"For our clients, we first determine if Facebook is the appropriate outlet and customize our approach based on our client's goals," says Mike Nierengarten, an Internet marketing consultant at Obility Consulting. "For example, our client Animation Mentor, an online animation school, is perfect for Facebook because it has tons of great content (video, events, and pictures), a strong (current) student presence on the site, and our target customers (potential students) use the site regularly."

But exactly how does one research an audience on Facebook? You can start by simply purchasing an ad on Facebook. As you go through the process, you'll learn more about your audience in terms of size and demographics. That said, I prefer the gumshoe method, meaning you log in and start looking. Demographics won't give you the insight into where people gather, what sort of messages they share, or the overall "vibe" of the community on Facebook interested in causes related to your organization's objectives. Any social media strategist worth his or her salt will tell you the first step in planning a strategy on social networks is to listen and you'll find the same advice here. Find active groups focused on relevant topics and join them. Spending most of your time listening and observing will give you the most valuable information you need to learn the most about your audience.

Determining Desired Outcomes

Once you have an idea who your audience is and what your goals are, you should consider what your desired outcomes are. Do you want to use Facebook to develop relationships with media people and bloggers? Are you more interested in finding and engaging your enthusiasts within your marketplace and building awareness among them? Do you have calls to action you'll measure, such as lead generation (for example, filling out a form), building website traffic, or generating conversation and buzz? Deliberate planning with your outcomes in mind is always a good idea.

Working with Bloggers and the Media

Virtual environments lend themselves well to building real relationships with media and bloggers.

Andrea Samacicia, founder and president of Victory Public Relations, a New York PR firm, told me that in her former life, several years ago when she was employed by another PR firm, she communicated with editors all day long, but didn't really start building real relationships with them until she started using social media. "I'm much closer to the people I interact with now," she says. "I have much closer relationships with the editors, producers, and journalists I'm linked to on Facebook and Twitter. It makes keeping in touch much simpler. You can "like" something they've done on Facebook and they get a little reminder about you."

In addition to building relationships and establishing another line of communication with key journalists and bloggers, by paying attention to what they share and post, you can learn more about what interests them and what they've written lately. You may even find a story opportunity among the interactions (see Figure 8.1).

You can even pitch media via Facebook — with some conditions.

"For the reporters in the Web 2.0 space, I have begun pitching them via Facebook. I have found they often respond quicker to my Facebook messages as opposed to the e-mails I send to their corporate accounts," says Andrew Miller, vice president, external communications at Integral Systems, in a discussion on LinkedIn. "Please note that I have relationships with these reporters and have linked to them on Facebook. For PR people interested in using Facebook as a means to pitch reporters, I suggest doing the same."

8.1 Subscribing to local journalists and bloggers gives you the opportunity to follow what they are posting and interact with them.

Finding and connecting with enthusiasts and influencers

There's something for everyone on the web, and on Facebook, or so it seems. For most organizations, Facebook represents a great opportunity to find and connect with "your people." Developing a presence people will want to connect and interact with requires the ability to produce, curate, and share interesting information and the willingness (and resources) to interact with your audiences one on one. Yes, you want to encourage people to like your Page. But building interactions with your content — getting people to like, share, and comment on the things your organization posts — is where the Facebook magic happens. Those liking and sharing interactions can trigger viral distribution of your message. People won't like or share boring things, however, so sharing good stuff is an imperative.

Good old-fashioned promotion

Facebook is a great place to generate publicity — that's obvious. Once you've done your research, identified what your audience likes, developed the content plan, attracted and kept your audience's attention, and have been rewarded with a growing following, then you can actually start to promote your company. Please note — promoting the company comes after you do all the heavy lifting described above. Building context — and communicating within that context — is important on social channels. It would be jarring — and uninviting — if a friendly, funny brand presence suddenly switched to the hard-sell.

That said, I do believe that people understand that brands need to promote themselves, and their products and services. And, let's face it — if you're in the market for a particular item, you're probably going to be interested in information related to that item. So it's perfectly okay to promote your business, brand, and products on Facebook. However, if you want to do so effectively, most of your communications should be focused on building relationships and credibility with your audience. If 80 percent of your communications are consistently focused on educating and entertaining your audience, they'll tolerate 20 percent promotional content — as long as you maintain the context you've already built. So go ahead and promote your blog posts, white papers, and other promotional content, invite your audience to special events, and offer them special deals and discounts for being loyal fans.

Simply put, Facebook can be a terrific medium for public relations, as long as communicators respect the personal nature of interactions and care is taken to connect the right audience with a carefully thought-out media strategy.

Public Relations Gurus Share Their Insights

There is no better way to learn about what works and what doesn't work than to go right to the experts and ask them to share their experiences. I reached out to a couple of highly regarded public relations experts and asked them to share their thoughts on using Facebook to gain media attention. The following sections are written by them and tell some stories of successes and failures. As you will see, challenges always arise, but if you handle them correctly, you can overcome them to achieve great success.

Cheryl Snapp Conner, managing partner, Snapp Conner PR

At an awards ceremony, I found myself seated next to three of my most geeky and connected tech friends, who were in the midst of a spirited debate.

"I use LinkedIn for professional contacts."

"Twitter is for my hobbies and personal interests."

"Facebook is where I post and find the things related to friends."

Each had their strategies for sorting the various social networking mediums for maximum advantage. So whose strategy was best? In my opinion, they all were. Regardless of the conscious strategy for which medium to use for what focus, it's inevitable that PR can play a unique role in them all.

But if Facebook is considered by many or most to be first and foremost a medium for connecting and conversing with friends, where does the PR function come into play? Everybody can name at least a few individuals or companies who have used the Facebook platform to sell and promote in a way that grated, offended, and very literally lost them friends. What, then, are smart companies doing to leverage the PR opportunities of Facebook? It's a new playing field with very few rules. In the following sections, I share a few savvy examples.

PR for building a dialogue

Consider the case of CityDeals, a daily deal site comprised of several thousand merchants and tens of thousands of active customer participants. CityDeals had maintained a Facebook Page (multiple Pages, actually, to support its various regions) as a means of communicating extra deals and bargains to subscribing participants. It was an excellent means of putting new ideas in the News Feeds of willing listeners, and for many of them, far less intrusive than daily or weekly e-mails.

But the Facebook Page took on supremely important meaning in 2010 when the company hit a rough patch. In the midst of the bad economy, the company entered into a merger agreement with another firm, hoping to bring an economy of scale that would help both companies be better poised to succeed. But finding and closing the right deal left the company undercapitalized for a period of several months, resulting in past-due payments to a number of merchants.

Then — in a nightmare scenario — the planned merger failed. Merchants and consumers erupted in outrage as merchants who were owed money stopped honoring deals. Consumers holding purchased certificates feared a default. The press was rabid, even implying criminal liability. Competing deal sites leapt on the situation and played attack ads, mocking the company's strife. After a two-week period, however, a terrific solution emerged — one of the company's merchants, family entertainment conglomerate Seven Peaks, recognized that CityDeals had too much value to fail and acquired the assets of the flailing company. The company was solid. The remaining team was passionate about making the participants whole and starting anew to make the newly founded company and brand stronger than ever before.

But a big problem loomed — hundreds of merchants needed to be settled with individually to determine suitable outcomes for the monies they were owed, and to determine if they'd remain with CityDeals going forward. At the same time, consumers were rabid with worry and anger that the certificates they were holding would expire or not be honored and they would be caught without a means of refund. It was a veritable PR nightmare.

In the press, CityDeals and its new owner announced and assured the public and community that it would do its best to move forward and make everyone whole by ensuring all deals were honored.

Facebook became the means of carrying forward a meaningful dialogue over the painful days and weeks in which the staff worked nearly round the clock to reach merchants and negotiate solutions one at a time.

With customer support lines and e-mail able to handle only limited questions (and every customer support call further slowing the transition), Facebook became the forum to post daily, or sometimes even twice daily, lists of the merchants resolved and the new agreements on board.

"What about the Awful Waffle?" one customer wrote in a post. "It's my favorite and I'm holding three certificates that are about to expire."

Facebook was the perfect medium to provide a quick answer to all: "They're on our list for this week. We are close to an agreement. We believe they'll be on board and accepting coupons again by next week."

"The Cookie Palace doesn't appear to be renewing. How can I get a refund?"

"The Sandy location is accepting coupons. You can redeem your coupons at that site, or you can e-mail your expired certificates to us for a credit or refund."

Accusatory comments were met with patience, candor, and even humor. Facebook became the medium that helped to quell the anger, communicate opportunity and reason, and ultimately complete a transition that has made the company stronger than before (and has made its participating constituents far more engaged.). This situation, which at times was actually crisis control, was an ideal scenario for putting Facebook to excellent PR use. Kudos to CityDeal for innovating a superb Facebook strategy for PR on the fly.

An interesting side note and caveat: When tempers were high, CityDeals avoided the temptation to censor or remove user comments. The company attempted to answer all questions, even the really unfair ones, with candor and grace. Only when the transition was nearly complete did the company post a cautionary note that from there forward, comments that were clearly meant to incite argument would be removed.

In contrast, another daily deal site experiencing difficulty attempted to use its Facebook Page to malign CityDeals and others. All comments or posts that didn't support this company's position quickly disappeared. The company removed them by monitoring the site closely and reporting to Facebook any remark it didn't like as "spam." Instant result: comment gone. The censorship was a mistake that backfired, and the firm suffered irreparable PR harm.

PR for building a following

Not every PR use of Facebook involves crisis control. For example, Mountain Resorts, a branded vacation rental website from Salt Lake City–based VacationRoost, used Facebook to build a following of more than 13,000 prospective visitors and customers within a matter of weeks. How?

By offering swag. The company did a limited amount of Facebook advertising, which gave it some momentum. But far and away, the company gained its highest traction by offering prizes — mostly vacation travel prizes, in keeping with the company's service and theme — via weekly drawings. Sound bland? Not for this company — the weekly drawing was filmed and broadcast live, every Friday morning, via Facebook, of course. There was no clever performance; no viral production involved — simply the genuine action of drawing and announcing a winner that captured interest and showed all participants that the contest was very real. The broadcast remained online via a YouTube video, so it was present for any viewers in the Facebook News Feed, whether or not they happened to catch it live.

Wilson Electronics of Saint George, Utah, is another company that's used Facebook (and Twitter) as a powerful strategic weapon (see Figure 8.2).

Wilson ran contests, soliciting creative videos from followers and inviting them to provide links on Facebook and Twitter to show the world their results. The response was phenomenal, building thousands of followers over the course of a few weeks.

8.2 Wilson Electronics successfully used Facebook as a strategic weapon to gain positive PR and increase its marketing reach.

Consider also the way journalists such as eWeek's Wayne Rash and the *New York Times's* David Pogue use Facebook to build the subscribership for their columns and articles. After each Wayne Rash column (on the failure of the AT&T and T-Mobile merger, for example), Wayne posts a link to the column as a status update on Facebook. However, it's not *just* a link to his article — in the informal Facebook forum, he's able to provide a bit of extra commentary, aside from the published article, that gives readers the chance to hear his candid opinions in a way that's more personal.

David Pogue uses this strategy to highlight product opinions and reviews from his *New York Times* articles as well as his feature projects such as a recent segment on PBS, where his traditional readers would not have expected him to be.

The extra effort by a writer or columnist pays off in many respects — emerging new publications such as *ITBusinessEdge* and *CTOEdge,* for example, choose their columnists based not only on the quality of perspective and writing, but on their ability to bring a following and a readership with them. Facebook is one of these columnists' primary tools.

Expanding the reach and the scope of a company's PR program

Fishbowl, a fast-growing inventory management software company in Orem, Utah, has used Facebook as a key mechanism to expand the reach and the scope of its company's PR.

The company excels in corporate responsibility. Facebook has been an ideal mechanism for communicating the progress of its Courage Above Mountains (CAM) foundation, which provides digital learning and support for single moms and other underserved individuals such as students in the Navajo Nation. Facebook is the means of spreading much of Fishbowl's communication to the community and partnering to invite them to join CAM's initiatives.

Many of the viral aspects of Fishbowl's public relations translate extremely well to the medium of Facebook. For example, the company recently garnered regional and national attention for its buyback from the prior majority investor. To make a strong point about financial prudence and careful use of debt, Fishbowl and its employees had an all-out push to prepay the $1 million bank note that had been a part of its buyback ahead of time, on the date of the first loan payment after a six-month period of interest-only payments on the company's loan.

At the celebration press conference, the company held a "dance off." Egged on by the exuberant employees, the CEO was persuaded to join in the dance, and jokingly danced across the room, ending his performance on one knee, in a bodybuilding pose (Fishbowl also places a high priority on fitness). The cameras were rolling and the CEO's dance made the regional news, even going viral through Facebook posts and reposts. The company's website viewers went wild with response to the news as well as to the video.

A large firm that was finalizing a purchase of competing software learned about Fishbowl from the video segment. It halted everything and sought out Fishbowl, saying, "We need to find out more about this unique company before we make our software decision. Tell us some more."

This was a PR outcome far beyond what the company had anticipated, but the viral and personal nature of Facebook helped substantially in bringing about this outcome.

Mistakes to avoid

Not every PR use of Facebook is a good one. Individuals and companies who use their Facebook presence as a chance to constantly and blatantly promote bear the consequences — connected individuals disconnect and feel annoyed and confronted by the unwelcome intrusion into their space and their time.

A jewelry designer went so far as to post advertisements for new pieces on its followers' Walls (now called Timelines). Affronted, many of those users went beyond simply ignoring the ad — they were irritated enough to disconnect, to hide the company, and in some cases even to report the company to Facebook for proliferating spam. Not a good PR outcome.

Consider the audience and the forum. Friends in a private group who discuss fitness and workouts are somewhat affronted to see repeated posts from one of the group members about press appearances and columns she's published on parenting skills. If the post is not at all in line with the theme of the group, many members are affronted by the blatant misuse of the "captive audience" there.

Another sensitivity to consider: When you post an announcement or piece of information about a company, many readers or viewers consider it an important piece of PR protocol to also disclose any working relationship there. For example, if a PR firm posts the good news about a client's achievement, the post should clearly refer to the firm in question as a client, to avoid raising the hackles of readers who consider that information a critical part of the honesty and background of what the poster has said.

With these nuances in mind, it's possible to use Facebook as a forum for advancing PR in new and unique ways. As with any tool, consider the medium and use it wisely and with integrity for maximum PR results.

Janet Tyler, president, Airfoil Public Relations

Facebook takes a pulse on what's news, now. There are those who say that technology has done more to isolate than connect us, but these same individuals should consider how social networking channels like Facebook have actually enabled deeper, more mutually satisfying relationships between not only friends and family but also businesses and media. In fact, social platforms lend themselves well to building real relationships with media as long as communicators respect the personal nature of interactions and care is taken to connect the right audience with a carefully crafted message (see Figure 8.3).

179

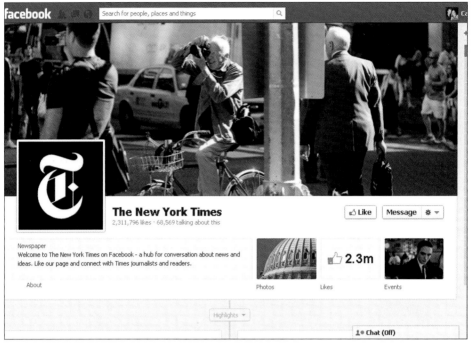

8.3 Local and national media are on Facebook, which allows them to connect and build relationships with your product or business.

Airfoil has worked with successful global enterprises, including Microsoft, eBay, and LinkedIn, to leverage social media to engage with media, bloggers, analysts, and customers. Our experience is that clients that approach Facebook as an interactive medium, as opposed to a static billboard, derive the greatest return on investment for their efforts. Even a global brand with thousands of "friends" won't generate quality audience engagement if its Facebook presence isn't nurtured, almost like a living, breathing entity.

Businesses of all sizes (even large ones with existing media relationships and traction) are challenged to fill the gaps caused by the receding of traditional media due to the proliferation of online content. On Facebook, a small business with limited PR resources can open an account for free and gain access to the same site features and networking potential as larger companies have. If small-business owners listen carefully to what their Facebook peers and media connections are saying, they can also optimize their time spent targeting reporters with story ideas. In this way, Facebook has leveled the public relations playing field for small and large businesses, while creating a new elastic media environment (see Figure 8.4).

180

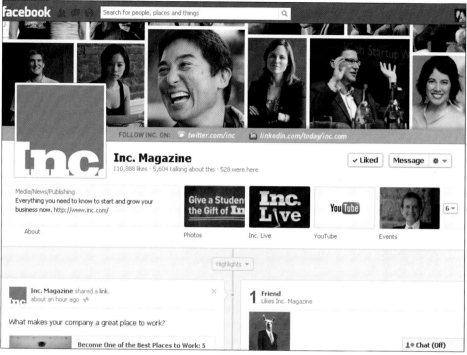

8.4 Following your peers and media sources can open you and your business to the trends being talked about and give you some of the same PR opportunities that large companies have.

Consider how the typical relationship between a member of the media and a business or public relations professional plays out:

1. **A business develops a press release or a pitch and cycles through necessary internal reviews, edits, and approvals.** With every moment that passes, the story's relevance diminishes.

2. **This same business (ideally) researches media contacts, using contacts' reporting focus or prior coverage as criteria for targeting.** More time passes, with the media landscape — reporter assignments and editorial hierarchy — evolving at the same time.

3. **Someone on the business side hits send and media receive said "news."** Target reporters may have written a similar story appearing in yesterday's business section, or breaking news may cast an alternate light on the business story. If none of these variables changed, the news may get picked up, but lack of access to real-time information from media can also make one's news yesterday's story, in a heartbeat.

The primary flaw in traditional media relations — and always one of the public relations industry's greatest challenges — is that, while the process is linear, news by definition rarely is. And it's this gap between what businesses want to say and the timely news criteria media require that makes Facebook a smart, effective media relations tool in today's blink-and-you-miss-it world.

Social media channels like Facebook have enjoyed enormous popularity because of their ability to customize, intensify, and accelerate communications. Facebook connections between business owner and editor or reporter (which, in a perfect world, are reciprocated) can generate more meaningful business communication results than blind copying a database full of "targeted" media contacts and blast e-mailing an announcement.

Making friends with media

To take full advantage of Facebook's media relations value, all businesses must recognize that there is a very specific protocol to initiating contact with media through this medium. In typical media relations, businesses and their communicators most often make initial contact through phone or e-mail without prior introduction to that contact. Certainly there are instances where media connections are made at networking events or via a mutual acquaintance, but in most cases, media accept and expect that at any given moment during the work day a relative stranger will simultaneously introduce himself and ask the reporter to cover his company's story.

On Facebook there is a higher standard for familiarity. Whereas media aren't gatekeepers of their e-mail and voicemail accounts, on Facebook they do hold the key — by way of accepting (or ignoring) a friend request — to developing a one-to-one relationship. Just as individuals do not typically friend strangers on Facebook, business communicators should not attempt to friend media with whom they do not have some existing relationship. This is a critical difference in offline and social media relations, and this barrier to entry can actually heighten the quality of media interactions by ensuring that businesses focus their outreach and media receive information from trusted, valued sources.

An exception to this rule is Facebook's Subscribe button, where businesses or individuals can follow people they find interesting but with whom they are not formally acquainted. Facebook Subscribe doesn't allow two-way communication, but it does enable subscribers to receive updates from their favorite reporters or bloggers right in their News Feeds (see Figure 8.5).

However, remembering the rules of media engagement on Facebook, business market-ers should not attempt to contact a subscribed member of the media directly should they want to follow up on something posted in a News Feed. Rather, marketers should use a different medium (such as a phone call or e-mail) to let these contacts know that they have something of value to add to a Facebook post and initiate first contact in this manner. Should all go well, these marketers may be able to progress to friending media after initial introductions.

Subscribe button

8.5 The Subscribe button allows you to follow an individual without friending them.

Marketers must push and pull the story

After the introductions and friending occur, businesses often find that the natural flow of information exchange on Facebook effectively streamlines the rest of the media rela-tions process through this channel. Similar to nonsocial media relations, businesses that both *push* news (through direct outreach) and *pull* leads (by tracking a reporter's status updates) on Facebook increase their odds of securing coverage and, perhaps more importantly, gaining the trust of target media.

Of course, in social media, a push becomes a pull and vice versa, but the premise is the same. Facebook is a powerful tool for giving and receiving information. The channel lends itself well to various outbound and inbound media relations activities, some of which are listed here:

- **Push (or outbound) media relations:**

  - Businesses on Facebook have a built-in news distribution tool, where company updates and information can be disseminated in near real time. If media have liked your Page, they may identify a status update as a bona fide lead. This approach to push media relations is becoming more effective as journalists are increasingly using Facebook to identify story sources, and it also ideally turns into a "pull" tactic with interested reporters.

  - One of the most valuable insights gained from connecting with media on Facebook is updated information on what they're reporting. In some instances, a business may have a strategic counterpoint to make or additional perspective or data to provide. Facebook is an ideal platform for starting a conversation around the other sides of a story and possibly leading to complementary coverage.

  - Depending on the level of "friendship" with an outlet, marketers can send pitches via Facebook's internal e-mail system, which may break through the noise of traditional e-mails. However, marketers must be careful to preserve trust with their media Facebook connections and only do this if it's confirmed that the contact is open to receiving pitches this way. Some media may use Facebook for only personal interactions and prefer that business communications take place elsewhere.

- **Pull (or inbound) media relations:**

  - Business marketers should keep in mind that social media is dynamic. Its very nature requires the giving and taking of information. In addition to posting company news as status updates, marketers should use Facebook to gain a deeper understanding of reporters' preferences, personalities, and passions. When a marketer interacts with a reporter in a natural and personal way, that reporter may not be more apt to deem the marketer's press release newsworthy (it either is or it isn't), but he or she may be more apt to reach out to the business seeking sources or to test story concepts.

- Status updates can be used by marketers to not only promote news but to highlight the company's leaders and their respective experience and opinions. Marketers can establish a cadence for posting company leadership "spotlights" in their status updates to essentially market resident subject matter experts to any media in their network and increase likelihood of an inbound request for comment.

Some media relations activities qualify as neither push nor pull, but they can be effective at building relationships nonetheless. For example, liking a reporter's status update is an unobtrusive way to gain awareness with that media contact. Also, if a business holds a close relationship with a member of the media, Facebook can be an excellent medium for brainstorming story angles with that contact or even peers or acquaintances in public relations.

The key is for small businesses to take full advantage of the dynamic nature of social media, use that fluidity to build personal, strategic relationships with media, and recognize status updates as rich opportunities to identify and nurture story ideas. While making the connections on Facebook does require finesse, once made, "friendships" between businesses and media can assume an even more authentic feel than those formed in the offline world.

| Timeline | Info | Photos | Notes |

Leveraging Facebook as a Platform

Your website is a crucial part of your online marketing, overall identity, and sales efforts. Without a website, you cannot compete in today's marketplace. When you have a website, customers can find your products and services through search engines and use your site as a powerful resource for information on what you sell.

Smart businesses are going beyond just using Facebook to post comments and interact with customers — they are leveraging Facebook as a platform for enhanced communication and collaboration on their websites or other digital properties.

Why Platforms Are Important

As a small business owner, you want to focus on selling your products, supporting your customers, and growing your business. However, you are not an expert in everything. You must work with a lawyer to draft contracts, an accountant to do taxes and manage cash flow, an office space consultant to design your office, and other experts to help with many other things.

You also must connect with customers on mobile devices and through social media. Instead of you creating and maintaining all the services your company needs, larger companies, such as Facebook, provide ecosystems of services. You don't have to build an infrastructure to connect with your customers; you can leverage Facebook — a platform — for this.

Here is one nontech example. Sure, you could store money in your home, under the pillow or in a safe. But when everyone pools money in a bank, the bank can provide services leveraging all the money in its care. Similarly, using a technology platform is more powerful than relying only on your website. Technology platforms have built-in features (such as Check-in Deals, location services, and the ability to indicate if colleagues are online and available for communicating) and large numbers of users.

Sure, you could hire a programmer to develop one or more of these services. But by using the platform of a larger infrastructure (such as Facebook), you save development time and money and take advantage of the pool of potential and current customers already on the platform.

Although many of the tools platforms offer out of the box are interesting, companies can also "mash up," or combine, the tools or features of the service or of other services to make something uniquely beneficial to the business.

For example, the soft serve retailer Tasti D-Lite linked its loyalty cards with its social media sites, including Facebook. Every time Tasti D-Lite customers used their loyalty cards, their friends were automatically alerted on Facebook or on sites that they linked with their loyalty card — friends would see a post on their Facebook Wall (now the Timeline) or a tweet in their Twitter feed. Customers who linked their loyalty cards to their social network got more loyalty points. Pretty innovative! You can watch my interview with BJ Emerson, vice president of technology at Tasti D-Lite, at http://bit.ly/hnxgWa.

This is the power of using Facebook as a platform in your business. Phil Simon's book, *The Age of the Platform* (www.theageoftheplatform.com) is good reading for more on this issue.

Integrating Facebook and Your Website

Social networks have become so popular because they connect people with one another. Traditional websites don't have social connectivity built in to them. Sure, you can comment on a blog post and see what others have commented on, and there are other things you can program into your website. But Facebook's natural social connectivity makes it much easier to ensure your website connects your users around your brand and its online content (see Figure 9.1).

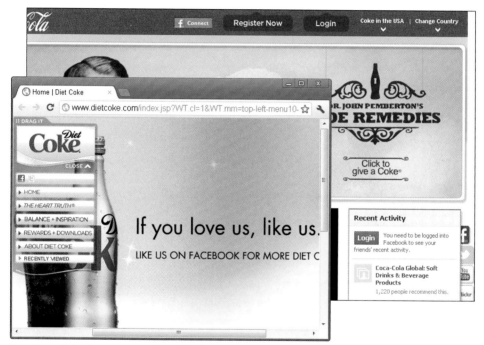

9.1 Coca-Cola does an amazing job of integrating social plug-ins with its website. It makes good use of the News Feed and the Connect and Like buttons to encourage customers to interact with the website, Facebook Page, and products.

There are three key pillars of integrating Facebook's platform into your website:

- Social plug-ins
- Authentication
- Personalization

Social plug-ins

Many small-business websites get very little traffic compared to those of big national brands. By adding a social plug-in to your website, you provide online visitors with instant comfort and the validation of seeing who else in their networks are also reading or otherwise engaging with the website.

Examinations of companies who have started using social plug-ins have indicated that their overall traffic and user engagement have increased.

It's pretty easy to add a Like button to your website (see Figure 9.2):

1. **Visit https://developers.facebook.com/docs/reference/plugins/like.**

2. **Scroll down until you see the Get Like Button Code form and type the URL of your Facebook Page into the URL to Like text box.**

3. **Select a layout style from the Layout Syle drop-down list.** You can choose between standard, button_count, and box_count. Each style can be previewed in the open box to the right.

4. **Enter the width in the Width text box.**

5. **Select the Show Faces check box if you want to show the profile photo of those who have liked the Page.**

6. **Select the verb you want displayed, either "like" or "recommend."**

7. **Select the color scheme of the plug-in, either light or dark.** Again, each choice can be previewed by selecting the option and viewing it in the open box to the right.

8. **Choose the font that you want to use in the plug-in.** There are multiple choices and each can be previewed by clicking it and viewing it in the open box to the right.

9. **Click Get Code to retrieve the code for the plug-in.**

You'll then be given HTML code that you can copy and paste into your website content management system.

facebook DEVELOPERS | Search 🔍 | **Documentation** **Support** **Blog** **Apps**

Like Box
Like Button
Live Stream
Login Button
Recommendations Box
Registration
Send Button
Subscribe Button

Beta Plugins

Recommendations Bar

Step 1 - Get Like Button Code

URL to Like (?)

[   ]

👍 Like 171k 💬 Send

Send Button (XFBML Only) (?)
☑ Send Button

Layout Style (?)
[button_count ▼]

Width (?)
[450]

Show Faces (?)
☑ Show faces

Verb to display (?)
[like ▼]

Color Scheme (?)
[dark ▼]

Font (?)
[▼]

[**Get Code**]

9.2 Complete the simple form to create code for the Like button plug-in that can be inserted in your website.

There are a variety of social plug-ins that you can use with your website. Which one you use really depends on how you want your website visitors to interact with your Facebook Page and the design of your website.

Here are some of your options:

- **Send button.** The Send button enables your users to easily send your website address to their friends in a Facebook message.

- **Subscribe button.** The Subscribe button enables people to subscribe to your updates on Facebook. When a user subscribes, your posts and content appear in their News Feed.

- **Comments box.** The Comments box lets users comment on any piece of content on your site. If users leave the Post to Facebook check box selected when they post comments, those comments appear in their friends' News Feeds.

- **Activity Feed.** The Activity Feed plug-in shows users what their friends are doing on your site, such as likes and comments.

- **Recommendations box.** The Recommendations box gives users personalized suggestions for pages on your site they might like.

- **Like box.** The Like box enables users to like your Facebook Page, see the number of users who already like the Page and who among those users they are friends with, and read current updates from the Page.

- **Login button.** This plug-in shows profile pictures of the user's friends who have already signed up for your site in addition to a Login button.

- **Registration plug-in.** The Registration plug-in allows users to easily sign up for your website with their Facebook account. Say you have a website that requires users to register to access information. Instead of having users type in registration information (such as an e-mail address), the registration plug-in lets them register by typing in their Facebook e-mail address and password.

- **Facepile plug-in.** The Facepile plug-in displays the Facebook profile pictures of users who have liked your Page or have signed up for your site.

- **Live Stream plug-in.** The Live Stream plug-in lets your users share activity and comments in real time as they interact during a live event.

Authentication

On your website, you want users to authenticate themselves and indicate who they are. Sure, you could develop your own system and ask users for lots of information and verify their e-mail address. However, Facebook allows your visitors to log on to your website (or other online content) using their Facebook logon information.

Using this part of Facebook might require a programmer to help you integrate the code into your website.

According to Facebook, there are three steps to the complete authentication process: "In order to log the user in to your site, three things need to happen. First, Facebook needs to authenticate the user. This ensures that the user is who they say they are. Second, Facebook needs to authenticate your website. This ensures that users are giving their information to your site and not someone else's. Lastly, users must explicitly authorize your website to access their information. This ensures that users know exactly what data they are disclosing."

The authentication feature of Facebook is tremendous. Instead of asking your users to fill in information about themselves, you can obtain their basic information with their permission through Facebook. This information includes their ID, name, picture, gender, and locale.

Personalization

Another way that you can leverage the power of Facebook for your business is to personalize your website for each user, depending on his or her logon information. Part of this personalization is publishing things to the users' Facebook Timeline and News Feeds. This means that not only are you engaging with particular online users but they are also your mini-evangelists telling their Facebook friends about content on your website.

Apps and Mobility

Many companies are finding success in leveraging Facebook's platform by creating apps that customers and prospective customers can leverage to enhance their customer experience with the company. This might include something for productivity, such as a tracking and shipping application within Facebook, or something more fun, such as a game related to the product or service you sell. This all happens within Facebook.

Overall, apps are a great way to not only engage your customers but also provide information to the network of your customers, encouraging digital referrals and word of mouth about your brand.

These are just some of the ways that apps can be used to extend your reach and engagement to customers and prospective customers. Check out Chapter 10 for more information.

Designing for Community

Prior to social networks, websites and e-mail newsletters were designed as one-way communication mechanisms. They were thought of as digital brochures at the least and online megaphones at most.

With the advent of social networks, in particular Facebook, web designers have been challenged to ensure their websites are not only filled with great content for their users but also enable customers to connect with other customers and facilitate engagement and conversation.

Quote, Unquote: Utilizing Community

"Utilize Facebook profile data in your app. If users grant the required set of permissions, you can utilize the Graph API to access users' likes, interests, activities, movies, and more to recommend content in your app. In addition, you can also access their friends' likes to suggest content they may be interested in. Users have spent a lot of time curating their Facebook profiles, so using that information effectively can drastically enhance their experience, provided you clearly communicate how you are using it."

Source: https://developers.facebook.com/socialdesign/personalize

Your customers are for sure speaking about you online — they're praising your new product or flaming the bad service they got from your new hire. By being proactive and facilitating these conversations, you can at least be one of the first to discuss what's happening at your company specifically or overall in your industry.

Say you operate a small bed-and-breakfast and want to go beyond just posting pictures of your rooms. By having a website designed for community, you can leverage Facebook (working with a programmer to help you) and help users find the best room for them based on recommendations of other users.

Case Study: Leveraging the Facebook Platform to Raise Brand Awareness

Here's one example of how a company, Hiscox Insurance, used Facebook to promote and manage a contest.

In the fall of 2011, small-business specialist insurer Hiscox launched a contest on Facebook called MyStartupStory. The purpose of the contest was to collect from entrepreneurs and small-business owners their start-up stories, best advice, and lessons learned when they first launched their business.

Objective

The objective of the contest was to help maintain and increase brand awareness of Hiscox in the United States, because although Hiscox has a strong U.K. brand and a 100-year history, the company is a new entrant in the U.S. small-business space. By combining interactive content on Facebook as well as other social media platforms, including Twitter and LinkedIn, Hiscox engaged with current and potential customers, increased interaction with current followers, and attracted new followers.

Execution

The Hiscox MyStartupStory contest was conducted from September 27 through November 11, 2011, and asked passionate entrepreneurs and small-business owners to create either a 2- to 5-minute video or a written essay describing their start-up story for a chance to win $10,000 and other prizes. Entrants shared their advice for other small businesses, including the biggest challenges they faced, how they overcame them, the best advice they received, and the biggest lesson they learned in the process.

Strategy

Hiscox planned a multipronged media strategy to promote the contest:

- A blast e-mail was sent by Hiscox to current clients to encourage their participation.

- A description of the contest was posted to Facebook and that link was tweeted to followers.

- A media alert about the contest was posted to Hiscox's website, which was linked to via Twitter and the Facebook Page to drive participants to the Hiscox site.

- The contest was promoted daily via social media channels to drive the participation rate.

- Hiscox reached out to bloggers and Twitter influencers to assist in the promotion.

- Entries were posted on the Hiscox blog as ongoing promotion for both the contestants and the contest itself.

- The submissions were sent through the Facebook Page and monitored by Hiscox on the back end.

Hiscox chose to execute the contest on Facebook because of the reach and flexibility the platform affords. Hiscox was able to both run the contest from Facebook and promote the entrants and winners through its Facebook Page. Most concerted social media activity before the contest was focused on Twitter, and Hiscox was able to use that growing following and cross-promote the contest on Facebook, which until then had been a less-utilized platform.

Cost

Hiscox used online survey service Wildfire App for Facebook Marketing to execute the contest. Wildfire charged a $5 initial fee and an ongoing fee of 99 cents per day. In addition to the nominal execution fee, Hiscox also provided a $10,000 grand prize to the winner and an option of items from Hiscox's "Supply Closet" (which included business essentials such as a paper shredder, an office chair, and an iPad, among others) to the second-place winner. The third-place winner received registration for a small-business conference (chosen from a list provided by Hiscox). In total, the cost for the contest and prizes was approximately $11,550.

Success and results

The cross-promotion on many social media platforms as well as a targeted media strategy garnered more than 70 submissions from small-business owners across 19 industries ranging from IT to health and wellness. The winning submissions were featured on the Hiscox Small Business Insurance Facebook Page until November 30, 2011.

In terms of measureable results, the MyStartupStory contest had the following impact across social and earned media channels:

- Post views increased 34 percent.
- Post feedback (comments and likes on the posts) increased 150 percent.
- New likes on Facebook increased 239 percent.
- Active users increased 134 percent.
- Twitter followers increased 152 percent.
- Seven articles were published in a variety of small-business outlets promoting the contest and directing people to the Hiscox Small Business Insurance Facebook Page. These publications had total reach of more than 400,000 based on circulation.

You can learn several lessons from this case study:

- It is imperative to do the majority of the legwork beforehand. Before launching, pay close attention to Facebook's contest rules and execute a thorough review of different contest vendors and contest plan options to ensure clarity on what is required versus what is prohibited and what to expect overall.

- Draft the questions in the submission criteria carefully to ensure you can elicit the proper tone and content from submissions.

- Make things as easy as possible for applicants. Hiscox found that allowing applicants to submit either a written or video entry allowed busy entrepreneurs who may not have time to film and edit a video to participate.

The MyStartupStory contest was an opportunity for entrepreneurs to share their real-world experiences with others, and Hiscox was encouraged by all the great stories and practical advice it received. Overall, the contest was a great success and enabled Hiscox to forge relationships with the entrants and winners of the contest, and even to leverage the winners for other business opportunities and referrals.

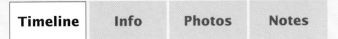

chapter 10

Creating and Using Facebook Apps

Just about everyone has heard of apps. With regard to Facebook, apps extend Facebook's capabilities. They can add life and functionality to your business's Facebook Page. The right apps also increase sales and engagement by giving you more powerful tools. You might want to consider hiring an app developer to make a custom app for your business.

This chapter explains what Facebook apps are all about, helps you evaluate whether you should create an app, and reviews Facebook's app approval policy. It also covers marketing and maintaining your app. Last, this chapter reviews third-party applications that can help your business.

Facebook Apps for Your Business 101

Apps, short for *applications,* are light-duty software codes meant to accomplish a particular task for the user. You have seen apps if you own a smartphone. In fact, apps have become serious business as the popularity of smartphones and tablets has increased substantially. A Kleiner Perkins Caulfield & Byers report (February 2011) noted a significant inflection point on the sales of tablets and smartphones over standard computers. This change in purchase behaviors has led to more demand for apps that are interactive and help accomplish errands and tasks. Facebook, a platform that is often accessed while on the go, is not immune to the app demand.

Like those used on a smartphone or tablet, Facebook apps are meant to accomplish tasks or entertain, but they do so within the Facebook platform. Facebook has developed apps that manage the additional features of a user's account. These apps include photo sharing, videos, static HTML, and notes.

Many third-party developers have also built apps for Facebook. The most successful are entertainment apps, such as Texas HoldEm Poker, CityVille, FarmVille, and Mafia Wars (see Figure 10.1).

This section focuses on apps that can improve your business operations and helps you decide whether to create apps designed specifically for your business and customers.

Discovering apps

Many Facebook users add newly discovered apps to their Pages without a second thought. In most cases, the discovery comes through a recommendation from a friend, a connection, or a trusted source.

Most of the top downloaded apps are games. These offer a casual escape from life that many Facebook users are seeking. So there is a tremendous interest in casual apps that may make a search for business app appear to be a bit of an Easter egg hunt. However, discovering business apps is possible.

10.1 One of the best-known apps on Facebook is FarmVille, a casual simulation game that has ordinary people tending crops at all hours of the day.

First, take inventory of the apps your account is already using. If you are interested in verifying an app within a Page, click Edit Page, and then click the Apps category to display a list of the apps you have added to your Page, each accompanied by a short description (see Figure 10.2).

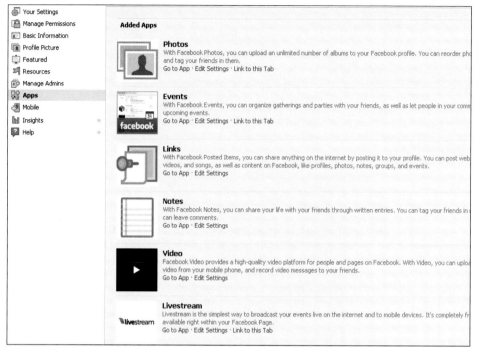

10.2 By clicking Edit Page and then clicking the Apps link in the left column, you can see the apps that are already applied to your Page along with a brief description.

Second, you can simply search for an app if you already know the name and might be interested in adding it to your account (see Figure 10.3). Type the name in the search box on your main Facebook Page. Typically, Facebook returns search queries according to group categories — apps, games, people, and Pages, for example — so it will be easy to identify the app. Click See more results at the bottom of the menu to see the complete search results. Click the app name that appears to display the app's home page. Apps vary on how they are accessed, although most have specific instructions for incorporating the app into the Page.

10.3 Using the search query bar, you can look for apps you may know by name or even type a category, such as e-commerce, to see what apps are available.

Another source for business apps is a third-party site called AppBistro (http://appbistro. com). AppBistro is specifically focused on business apps. When you log in with your Facebook Page, it syncs with your Page and information to suggest business apps that may benefit your business (see Figure 10.4). The apps are rated and reviewed for quality assurance. Screenshots are included with each application, along with instruction and, in some cases, tutorial videos.

TIP Don't crowd your Page with too many apps. Your Page is like a store: If there's not enough merchandise, then customers won't shop. Too much merchandise and customers get crowded out.

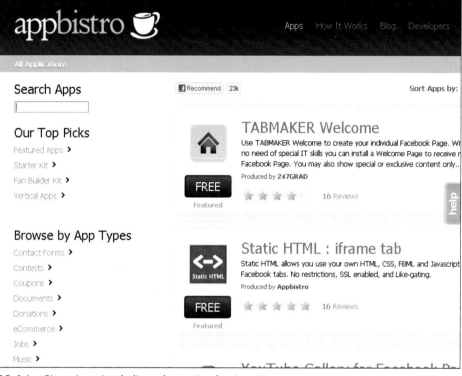

10.4 AppBistro is a site dedicated to rating business apps.

Using apps with your business

There are a number of ways you can use apps to grow your overall business. The key is assessing what types of services are part of your business's regular tasks, determining how these services are typically accessed by either customers or employees, and then seeing if the service offers a corresponding application.

If your business is reliant on the latest cloud software-as-a-service application, chances are a Facebook app version is available. For example, SlideShare is a popular online platform for sharing PowerPoint presentations, and a SlideShare app is available to share PowerPoint within Facebook (see Figure 10.5). NetworkedBlogs is another app that allows your blog posts to appear within the Facebook feed of your followers. This app lets you engage your Facebook fans and publish your blog simultaneously.

10.5 SlideShare is a great example of a business tool that also incorporates a Facebook app platform so you can integrate it into your Page.

Notice how many of these apps are republishing media that has been created and uploaded somewhere else, most often on the original software user interface. That is a significant operational benefit to your business. Apps help share media systematically, eliminating the extra work of uploading the information in several platforms. You should verify whether a Facebook app version of a favorite office tool is available to save you and your colleagues time in issuing supporting media of your products, services, and business. To do so, review the website of your preferred application — most sites note what application is available or even if one is being developed.

You may also want to assess the mobile capability of employees and customers as an aggregate. This can also affect where an application can be accessed. You can use a Facebook for Mobile page to review how a potential app user views and evaluate whether it is well designed and intuitive.

Top Facebook apps for business

Your Facebook Page can be greatly improved using third-party apps. Here are a few apps to start with. Also, search to see if your favorite application or online service has a Facebook app.

- **App Builder.** Create your own Facebook app without having to know any programming language (see Figure 10.6).

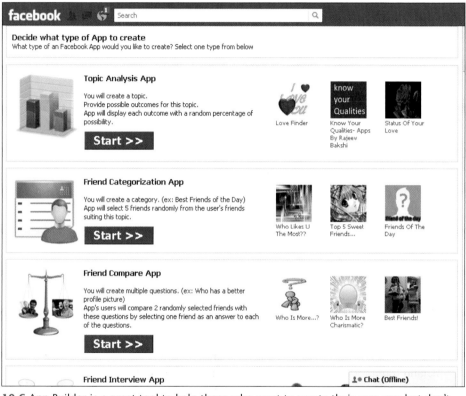

10.6 App Builder is a great tool to help those who want to create their own app but don't have the programming skills to do so on their own.

- **ContactMe.** This app adds a contact form app link in the views and apps section of your business's Facebook Page, making it easier for anyone who drops by to get in touch while his or her interest is fresh (see Figure 10.7).

10.7 ContactMe is a great app for adding a contact form to your business Page.

- **Easypromos.** This app allows you to add, manage, and modify promotions and competitions on your Facebook Page.

- **Extended Info.** This app gives you an app link in the views and apps section of your business Page that provides information beyond your default information, making room for deeper company details, such as information about products and services, in a customizable, media-rich format.

- **Huddle.** This app allows users to pull together shared workspaces, or *huddles*, using Facebook to connect with teammates and collaborators.

- **Endorse.** This app gives you a leg up with direct endorsements from within your Facebook community.

- **My Top Fans.** This app analyzes your interactions with followers to see who shares with you the most.

- **NutshellMail.** This app makes it possible to keep up with the swirl of communications by aggregating e-mail activity into a handy summary.

- **Pagemodo.** This app dresses up your Facebook Page with a simple template that enables you to easily jazz up fonts, photos, and other visuals.
- **Payvment E-Commerce Storefront.** This app can give you a rich e-commerce storefront on Facebook (see Figure 10.8).

10.8 If you are looking to incorporate a storefront to your Facebook Page, the Payvment app can definitely help you get started.

- **RSS Graffiti.** This app makes it easy to share blog posts, tweets, videos, and other social content with friends on Facebook, pushing out content with minimal effort.
- **SlideShare.** This app simplifies the task of sharing presentations, documents, videos, and webinars with your Facebook peeps as well as on LinkedIn.
- **Static FBML.** This app lets Facebook managers add new application tabs to their companies' fan Pages.
- **Tweets to Pages.** This app can help customers follow your Twitter feed more easily by displaying your most recent tweets in the Twitter app link in the views and apps section of your Facebook Page.
- **Twitter Feed for Pages.** This app pulls together tweets for a customized presentation on Facebook.
- **Wazala.** This app helps those without the technical chops mount a storefront quickly and easily (see Figure 10.9).

10.9 Wazala is another quick and easy app that lets you get a storefront up and running with little time and effort.

- **Work for Us.** This app streamlines human resources (HR), allowing you to post job openings and receive applications via your Facebook Page.

Should You Create a Facebook App?

You also have the option of creating an app specific to your needs or, more likely, to offer a version of your business services to your customers. An app specific to your business provides for an additional layer of engagement with potential customers. An app creates a way for customers to remember your business, and they will remember your business favorably if the app is helping them complete an essential task while mobile.

Another benefit to creating your own app is gaining income if you have traffic that numbers in thousands or more users per month. Advertising can be inserted alongside the app user interface. A number of client services can provide the means to serve ads during app usage. You can select the kind of advertising that can be served within the app format, but it should be from an approved provider. Facebook provides a list of approved advertising providers at http://developers.facebook.com/adproviders. You can also learn more about Facebook advertising guidelines at www.facebook.com/ad_guidelines.php.

To have an application built, begin searching the official developer source in Facebook. App developers are listed on the Facebook developer's page at http://developers. facebook.com/preferredmarketingdevelopers.

The other option is, of course, creating an application yourself. There are a few steps that you must undergo to set up the application.

You can begin creating a custom app for your business by going to www.facebook.com/ developers/createapp.php. The first time you access this site, the Developer app asks for permission to access your profile, and you must click Allow. The site then provides form fields that you need to complete to provide descriptions, icons, logos, the URL containing your privacy policy, and your canvas page.

An app is created within a canvas page. A *canvas page* is an iFrame within Facebook that allows users to interact with your application. Simply put, it is where people will interact with your application.

The canvas page is the unique location for your application in Facebook. When you decide on a name, it should be similar to the application name (letters, underscores, and dashes are permitted in the name, but numbers cannot be used). The canvas URL field holds the URL of the page on your server that hosts the application.

Another key aspect of your application is authentication. This is that pop-up box you see whenever you add an application to your Page that requires you to approve a transfer of information. The authorization should be designed to ask for only the minimal amount of information needed to operate the app. Be wary of developing an app that relies on personal identifiable information, as many users are concerned about providing personal information for no specific reason.

If you intend for your app to be used through a secure website, set it up so that your app users browse Facebook over an HTTPS connection. A Secure Canvas URL field in the Developer App enables developers to serve their apps through an HTTPS connection as well. This field is used to serve your app through an encrypted connection, if you (or your programmer) deem this necessary.

Here are a few other development tips to keep in mind for a well-planned app:

- **Create a great logo for your application.** A logo does not have to elaborate, but you must consider the idea that a logo can become a brand for your application. This is especially crucial in games but can also be the case for business apps as well.

Develop a solid description. Click the Auth Dialog category to see the Description field. A great description should state the benefit of the app's usage and be to the point. Like any product or service, an app should easily describe how it solves a user's need in a sentence or two.

 Show screenshots that clearly reveal what the app is about. Users who see descriptions of your app, particularly in sites like AppBistro, also want a visual representation of what to expect.

 Test the load time for your app. You should consider code that minimizes the number of server calls. This is especially a concern if the app is accessed through a mobile device. Try the web testing software NeoLoad (www.neotys. com/product/overview-neoload.html).

 Before you create your app, make sure you have a clear understanding of why you are creating it and the strategies you should implement to meet those goals.

App Approval and Policy

Once you've created and built the app, it is ready to go live, unless it's an Open Graph app, which must be approved by Facebook. Approval is submitted at the https://developers. facebook.com/apps page and is subject to how well your app meets the qualities covered in the following lists:

 Create a great user experience.

- Build social and engaging applications.
- Give users choice and control.
- Help users share expressive and relevant content.

 Be trustworthy.

- Respect privacy.
- Don't mislead, confuse, defraud, or surprise users.
- Don't spam. Encourage authentic communications.

To delve further into the qualities Facebook looks for in a new app, it provides a clear policy and guidelines site so that you, or the app developer, do not accidentally violate rules when creating and developing app code. The policy consists of 11 segments meant to address not only the application but also the use of services connected to the application, such as advertising and Facebook Credit usage. The site for the policy is at http://developers.facebook.com/policy, but the following segments have been highlighted:

211

I. Features and Functionality. This section covers how the app should function within the Facebook environment, such as providing a Facebook Log Out option on your app site. It includes special provisions for apps on Pages.

II. Storing and Using Data You Receive From Us. This section covers the management of data received from the Facebook API and user accounts, as well as how the data is processed.

III. Application Content. This section outlines responsibility for all content within your application, including advertisements and user-generated content. This states what is not to be promoted such as alcohol-related content (unless the appropriate demographic restrictions are used) or sale of tobacco products, ammunition, or firearms. It also covers content within advertisements and cross-promotions.

IV. Application Integration Points. This segment addresses the new user access and notification of an application. Integration points are places within Facebook where users can select your app and where they can receive notifications. The policy concerns outlined here make sure you are seeking consent and not inadvertently violating policies.

V. Enforcement. This explains the enforcement actions Facebook can take against applications that violate its Facebook Platform Terms and Policies.

VI. Changes. This is a straightforward mention that Facebook can change policy at any time without prior notice.

VII. Definitions. This section defines terms used within the policy.

VIII. Branding and Promotion Policy. This refers to the guidelines set forth in the Facebook Brand Permissions Center (www.facebook.com/brandpermissions/logos.php).

IX. Advertising Guidelines. Facebook has specific advertising guidelines, which are fully outlined, that must be followed to ensure that all ads contribute to and are consistent with the overall user experience.

X. Facebook Credits. This includes terms and guidelines meant for developers participating in the credit acceptance program.

XI. Ads API. This section addresses functionality between accounts and the Ads API.

Another resource to consider is the Future of Privacy Forum. This website shares information regarding data privacy within applications. You can use resources like this to keep you abreast of changes that would impact your application development. To learn more, go to www.applicationprivacy.org.

App Marketing

The main rule in creating an app is to develop a marketing plan at the same time the app is being developed. As mentioned previously, the growth of smartphones and tablets has created a competitive environment where launching an app without a plan is a plan for a languishing app. Facebook users are faced daily with new apps, creating a seemingly endless calculus in selecting the best apps to download.

This leads to a standard mistake businesses make: an overreliance on viral marketing for services and products offered in social network platforms as popular as Facebook. This mistake occurs when a budget is mostly dedicated for app development. Many businesses unwittingly approach the Internet as if any offer posted online is automatically known to the world. All someone has to do is issue the product and people will discover the offering by searching alone. This is not the case.

The Internet today is a wealth of choices and information. Experian noted in its 2011 Digital Marketer report that the majority of customers research prices online before making a purchase. However, the increasing adoption of the Internet into consumer lives has drawn virtually every business and increased interaction such that simply introducing a product is the equivalent of standing on a Manhattan street corner. Yes, people see you, but they are not going to stop and interact automatically because you are in front of them. Facebook can be the same way. It may have a highly engaged audience that remains on its property longer than on most sites, but it is an audience whose attention still needs to be earned. Plus, your offering has a customer target — by age, region, or demographic — so a Facebook audience that should be noticing your product should match your intended customer. Thus, while search is a standard Internet behavior, it requires some awareness building to initially gain traffic.

A budget is essential for successful marketing of an app. There are over 500,000 current apps within Facebook. Although a Facebook audience spends a higher-than-average amount on time on Facebook compared to most sites, many may not consider adding a new app. Thus, it can require marketing to augment any initial discovery of an app. Many companies, hearing of viral campaigns on the Internet, fail to budget a marketing effort, but it is clear that garnering attention online has become more than lightweight effort. This is particularly a concern if users are accessing your app via a mobile device.

You can market your app in your current marketing material and through your current marketing channels. Here are a few examples:

- Mention your app in your e-mail signature.
- Feature your app in an industry blog.
- Add a link in your newsletter to your Facebook app.

- Regularly tweet mentions of your app.
- Run a Facebook ad.
- Mention your app in your blog.
- Mention your app on your Facebook fan Page.
- Create a special app link in the views and apps section on your Facebook fan Page for the app.
- Run pay-per-click ads in other networks such as LinkedIn, Business.com, and on search engines such as Bing and Google.
- Create a specific press release on the app release.
- Mention your app availability on your website.
- Mention your app in your printed brochures.

There are also submission sites where your app can be listed.

AppData provides a submission page for including an app in its daily and monthly stat boards. It provides broad stat coverage for iOS as well as links to topic-specific sites (see Figure 10.10). You can use AppData as an alternative resource for app news and updates. It can also be a source to share app updates and news, though it must be kept in mind that the audience can be mainly developers in many cases.

Now, just because I urge you to create a marketing plan for your app doesn't mean your app cannot go viral in Facebook. An app can go viral, and many have. For example, CityVille, a popular game on Facebook, had nearly 300,000 users within 24 hours of its release (see *Facebook Marketing For Dummies,* Wiley, 2011). So while it does happen, I think it is necessary to take every viral success with a grain of salt. CityVille was developed by Zynga, which had immense previous success with Mafia Wars and FarmVille, two other highly popular Facebook games.

So how do you develop an app that spreads virally? The best initial results can come from energizing an intended audience prior to launching a product. It sounds easy but it can be a real challenge. Yet many companies succeed.

AppData ™

Independent, Accurate Application Metrics and Trends from Inside Network

Facebook Apps   iOS Apps

Home	Application and developer statistics from AllFacebook.com are now a part of AppData.com. To dig deeper on application and developer stats, choose an app, developer, or leaderboard below.
Leaderboards	

Top Applications

Top Developers

Gainers Today

Gainers This Week

Get Reports

Application Profile

Developer Profile

Compare Apps/Devs

Alerts and Feeds

Edit Email Alerts

Add Your App

Contact Us

Reports >> Leaderboards

List: Applications ▼ **By:** MAU ▼

For: February ▼ 22 ▼ 2012 ▼   Find

Filter by: Size Category

App Leaderboard   ✉ Add to My Email Alerts

	Name	MAU
1.	Static HTML: iframe tabs	87,200,000
2.	CityVille	46,800,000
3.	Static Iframe Tab	46,700,000
4.	Hidden Chronicles	33,400,000
5.	Texas HoldEm Poker	33,200,000
6.	BandPage by RootMusic	32,100,000

10.10 AppData provides great statistics on apps.

With respect to your app, try to energize your existing fan base in a similar manner. Give special teaser information, preview trials of products and services associated with your app, and give discounts to the most loyal users. Making your loyal users feel rewarded encourages them to share information about the app and create honest word-of-mouth marketing.

When you have released your app, you can ask for help from your audience. The trick is to make what you give is shareable so that the message can spread. If you know a few bloggers, provide a preview and ask if they can write about their first experience using the app. This can generate interest in the app that reaches out to a larger audience.

Also, ask your regular app users what they think about their first experiences using the app. Take time to listen and show that you are appreciative of their responses. The feedback will help guide your efforts to refine the app for future updates, which in turn is essential for continuing to attract new app users. Abandoning user feedback on an app sends an implicit message that your business does not care and your user base will diminish.

Also consider appearing and interacting on sites with more nuanced specialty topics than Facebook. This provides another audience who can download your app as well as learn about your business and other services. In some cases, seeking audience-specific sites can reinforce your position in your industry if influence among partners is important. A site like ReverbNation is a great example. ReverbNation is a LinkedIn for musicians and other music entertainment professionals. It provides social media features that allow artists to get the word out about their music. Your best strategic steps are to determine a way to consistently participate and work that network you have chosen. This could mean sharing blog posts or frequently posting on social networks to create a regular video show for your customers.

Most important, spend time to grow your initial launch audience while your app is in development, not when the app launches. Remember, a key marketing mistake is assuming visibility the instant an application is launched. To avoid it, begin building the number of your Page followers prior to an app's introduction. The larger the size your business Page becomes, the more favorable your chances for having information spread about your app and its subsequent updates.

TIP Just as you have a marketing plan for your business it's important to have a marketing plan for your Facebook app.

Facebook Ads for Apps

Using Facebook ads for apps can be very strategic. First and foremost, ads appear within Facebook, so it makes sense to take advantage of the Ads Manager. You can also target the ads to your intended app demographic as well as the region in which you want the ad to appear.

People who view your ad can see their friends who have used the app in the past 30 days. The app users are displayed as a mini-namepile alongside the ad. This name display provides social proof of content acceptance along with the advertising. The display of familiar faces makes ads more relevant to those who see it, leading to a potential increase in your click-through rates.

Keep in mind that social content regarding application usage only appears if the ad's destination URL starts with an app.facebook.com URL. This means that ads that mask the app URL won't have social content included. Tracking codes appended to the end of the app URL, such as that used for web analytics solutions, appear and function normally.

In addition, app users can adjust how their names are used in an ad if they want to opt out of having their names displayed.

App Maintenance

Your early app adopters will notice any bugs that may exist in your app. Depending on the audience, they may expect a few bugs and may not mind terribly. What is most important is how you respond to those bugs once they have been identified. Nothing says "I don't care" more than the nonresponse to app-user mentions. Pay attention to the comments from users about the app and spend time reviewing the trend in emotions expressed. Are app users becoming increasingly happy with usage, or are they increasingly frustrated?

Make sure there is a key place where your app developer or marketing team can monitor the comments and reply. Let app users know where they can send comments and observations. The business Page may be the most reasonable location, but keep in mind that comments can come from other sources, such as your blog or a Twitter feed. It may be necessary to monitor across platforms with a dashboard like Hootsuite or Postling to gain the best assessment of client app sentiment.

chapter 11

Timeline Info Photos Notes

Learning Lessons from Real Businesses

Maybe you think that marketing on Facebook is only for large businesses that can spend thousands of dollars to make it work. If so, you're wrong.

Facebook is an ideal platform for small businesses. It gives them opportunities to find new customers and engage current customers as never before.

This chapter provides examples of small businesses, such as Community Coffee and Squishable, that are succeeding in using Facebook, and it explains how they are doing it.

How Real Businesses Are Making Real Money on Facebook

Although Facebook started out as a platform for college students to connect with each other, it's now a place where real businesses are making money. This money can come from direct or indirect sales.

Successful businesses that use Facebook succeed for two main reasons: their content and advertising.

Content

Instead of blasting buy-from-me-now advertisements all over Facebook and to fans that like them, successful businesses provide rich content.

Think about how you and your own friends interact on Facebook. It's like a virtual coffee shop or living room get-together — you have fun and just relax. Businesses who share useful, insightful, or fun content that their fans want to receive become part of their fans' trusted community.

The stories that follow are about businesses that have been able to sell their products and services by being trusted sources to their online customers and prospective customers. Some businesses think leveraging Facebook is only for tech companies. It's not. Instead of trying to sell on Facebook, focus on your customers and give them an opportunity to share pictures, video, and other information for other customers to see.

Remember, what you post on Facebook is also important. Videos and photos are well received on Facebook. Aren't those the things you post in your own personal Facebook Page? Your customers are no different.

Advertising

You'll read in the following stories how companies purchased ads on Facebook and successfully boosted customer engagement or direct sales. Facebook advertising enables any business that knows its customers to find more of these customers online. Whether you decide to directly advertise to them or just get them to like your Facebook Page, Facebook advertising is a simple and effective way to attract more customers.

Every business owner should classify his or her business customers into distinct customer types. Facebook enables you to target your advertising based on the information in a person's profile instead of relying only on keywords. For example, say you want to target customers of a certain gender, age, and geographic location. You can do this with Facebook, which is why it's so powerful. But don't start by just selling a product. Use your money to attract an audience and identify customers who best resonate with your brand or what you are selling. Don't advertise women's shoes on sale. Instead, allow customers to post their favorite shoes and win a prize.

Overall, advertising on Facebook is different than advertising on TV or in the Yellow Pages. With Facebook you want your audience to *engage* with you. This is most important.

Analyzing Case Studies

To show you that it is possible to make real money on Facebook and create very successful marketing campaigns for very little money, I am sharing case studies of companies that achieved success with a little ingenuity and small budgets. Each company outlined in this section had a plan on how it wanted to use Facebook and was diligent in ensuring that its efforts and content remained current and in touch with its fan base. By doing so, each one saw results that can be achieved by any small business that is willing to put in the time and effort to promote its product and brand.

How Community Coffee builds a loyal customer community on Facebook

Who: This 91-year-old company began using Facebook as a way of reaching its niche customer base in the Southern United States.

What it did: Community Coffee used Facebook ads and its Page to build a community around its brand. One way it did this was tapping into fans' fond childhood memories and asking them if they drank coffee milk (a popular Southern treat) as children. It received overwhelming responses and engagement from fans.

The results: The Community Coffee Facebook Page has become one of the company's top five revenue generators (see Figure 11.1).

11.1 Community Coffee has over 187,000 fans that it can reach instantly to market its products.

How Squishable used Facebook ads to get more fans on Facebook

Who: Squishable is a company established in 2007 that makes unique stuffed animals for children and adults.

What it did: In 2009, Squishable began running Facebook ads encouraging people to like its Page (see Figure 11.2). Once on the Page, fans could invite friends to also become fans. Squishable rewards fans with coupons when the number of fans reaches certain milestones. This increases the likelihood a user will bring in more fans. Fans can browse the entire Squishable collection on the Page and go to http://squishable.com to purchase a stuffed animal.

Sponsored   Create an Ad

Squishable.com

They're giant round fuzzy stuffed T-Rexes. Hug them!

Like · 133,777 people like this.

11.2 By using Facebook ads, Squishable was able to reach a target audience and bring them back to its Facebook Page and website.

The results: Twenty-nine percent of Squishable's website traffic now comes from Facebook. Fans continue to regularly post pictures and videos of themselves with Squishable and ask for a new design, which helps to guide product innovation (see Figure 11.3).

facebook   Search   🔍

Squishable.com Squishable Voting! ▼   ✓ Liked

Vote for the next Squishable!

Squishable is a democracy! Your votes decide which animals get made into spherical form. Each time a design marathon comes around, Zoe takes the top 10 animals on the list and gives them her best Girl Scout try! If you feel strongly that the world needs a giant round Opossum, let your voice be heard! Vote!

Squishable White Tiger
+16138 👍 👎 -5304

Squishable Puffin
+16071 👍 👎 -7837

Squishable Cuttlefish
+12093 👍 👎 -4027

Squishable Crab
+14956 👍 👎 -6891

Squishable Nautilus
+12404 👍 👎 -4342

Squishable Sea Turtle
+11035 👍 👎 -3096

Squishable Beaver   👤 Chat (7)

11.3 Squishable fans and customers vote on what product they'd like to see next from the company, which truly allows the company to be in touch with what the customer wants.

This example shows the importance of knowing your audience. While blogs and websites are great tools, many businesses are finding that they can rely just on Facebook for a core part of their marketing, depending on who their audience is. Second, it's not enough to just beg for customers to buy from you or even visit your website. You have to reward them for the action and give them a reason to stay engaged (see Figure 11.4). The competition is only a mouse click away.

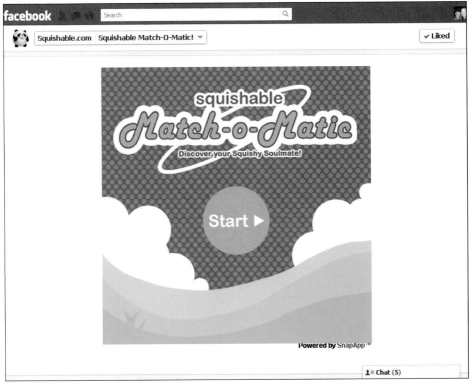

11.4 The Squishable Match-o-Matic pairs customers with their "Squishy soulmate." Engaging your customers, making them a part of your brand, and rewarding them for interaction are key ways to grow your Facebook fan Page and achieve marketing success.

How the company How Fast Time Flies used keyword targeting to boost sales

Who: Mom and entrepreneur Cathy Bennett launched her company, How Fast Time Flies, in 2007. It is an online scrapbooking service that offers a multitude of templates and the ability to share digital scrapbook pages online.

What it did: How Fast Time Flies began advertising on Facebook in 2009 to direct traffic and increase awareness of its digital scrapbooking service. Bennett said this about Facebook: "It's an enormously popular medium for moms to stay in touch with other moms, so that's a great audience for me to tap into." Bennett targeted keywords on Facebook to connect to those users interested in photography and scrapbooking.

The results: Year-over-year sales increased by more than 70 percent. Since the beginning of 2009, the company's website had received more than 200,000 visits from Facebook users.

How CM Photographics uses targeted Facebook ads to sell more photo services

Who: CM Photographics is a one-man wedding photography business based in Minnesota.

What it did: Owner Chris Meyer used Facebook ads to target his exact client demographic of local 24- to 30-year-old women whose relationship status on Facebook indicated that they were engaged (see Figure 11.5).

Recently engaged?

CM Photographics would love to be a part of your event. Mention this ad for $500 off!

11.5 By running Facebook ads targeting a very specific demographic, CM Photographics was able to generate incredible additional income for minimum cost.

The results: Over 12 months, CM Photographics generated nearly $40,000 in revenue directly from a $600 advertising investment.

How Wedding Paper Divas attracted engaged couples to buy wedding stationery

Who: Launched in 2006, Wedding Paper Divas is a haven for elegant stationery products and services (see Figure 11.6). Its main target is people who are in the market for wedding stationery.

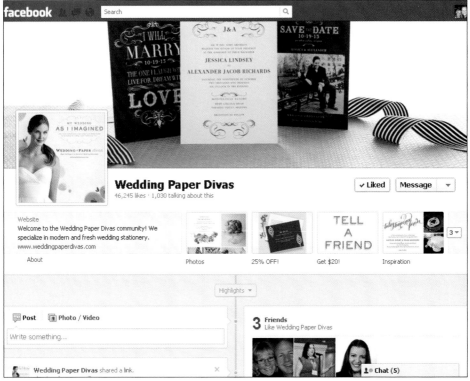

11.6 Wedding Paper Divas provides a specific product for a specific group of individuals.

What it did: Facebook ads provided Wedding Paper Divas the ability to target its exact demographic: 24- to 44-year-old women whose relationship status on Facebook indicated that they were engaged (see Figure 11.7).

The results: Wedding Paper Divas realized a 110 percent return on investment and saw a nearly 1 percent conversion rate from Facebook ads. Though the campaign ended, the return on its Facebook ads is still increasing. Conversions continue to occur as Facebook referrals return to complete purchases.

This case study illustrates how Facebook enables you to surgically target your audience across a variety of interests and demographics. The better you target your audience, the more effective you'll be in ensuring that the people most interested in your product or service see your advertisement.

11.7 By targeting a very specific demographic with a Facebook ad, Wedding Paper Divas saw a 110 percent return on investment.

How Thumbtack uses Facebook tools to sell services

Who: Thumbtack is a 12-employee San Francisco start-up that allows customers to find and secure various services, from artisans to carpenters.

What it did: Thumbtack has used three Facebook tools — Like buttons, an active Facebook Page, and Facebook Facepile — on its site. All have been used as a branding tool, said Sander Daniels, cofounder of Thumbtack. This is "so that people trust us more," Sanders said. "We're not a very well-known site, so anything we can do to show that your friends are using our site helps us!"

The results: Facebook helped Thumbtack monitor its services' rate of adoption (such as what services consumers engaging with the most). Facebook sends Thumbtack a weekly e-mail that includes key stats of all of its profile, such as number of visits, number of likes, and number of Timeline posts and comments. The e-mail also includes the rate of growth or decline for each of those stats. Thumbtack keeps a close eye on whether the number of weekly visitors, likes, and comments rises or falls each week.

How Pretzel Crisps boosted its likes in 36 hours using Facebook coupons

Who: Created in 2004 through a patent for a flat pretzel, Pretzel Crisps was developed by Sara and Warren Wilson, veterans of the snack food industry.

What it did: Pretzel Crisps wanted to drive fan growth on its Facebook Page via earned media. "Our social media strategy is to unite fans of our brand," said Jason Harty, director of field and interactive marketing for Pretzel Crisps.

The company also wanted to be nimble, cost efficient, and have the ability and relevancy to keep up with the conversation in relation to its Facebook presence. "One of our first priorities was to give value to our fans and use this added value to bring in new fans," said Harty.

Pretzel Crisps gained fans through a product trial (via coupons), providing fans a more rich experience and rewarding them for being a part of the community.

The results: Pretzel Crisps launched a $1 off coupon on Facebook during the last week of February 2011, and it saw fans grow from 6,800 to 13,700 in two weeks (see Figure 11.8). Since the launch, Pretzel Crisps has seen an 87 percent coupon redemption rate to date.

Then on March 15, 2011, Pretzel Crisps switched the $1 off coupon to a buy-one-get-one-free coupon. In a bit of an experiment, Pretzel Crisps did not tell anyone about the promotion. It wanted to see if it would spread with literally no push behind it — no status update, no advertising, no PR.

Within 36 hours, Pretzel Crisps had doubled its fan base on Facebook from 14,000 to 29,000. It now has more than 251,000 fans on Facebook and has seen these fans remain engaged on Facebook. The buy-one-get-one-free coupon has had a 95 percent redemption rate since it was introduced.

According to data from research firm SymphonyIRI Group, Pretzel Crisps increased its sales significantly in 2011 after this promotion. It's safe to say that part of Pretzel Crisps' phenomenal sales growth can be attributed to social media marketing strategy and tactics such as the Facebook coupons.

228

11.8 Pretzel Crisps launched a coupon campaign on Facebook and saw its fan base more than double in two weeks.

How Sweet Poppin's gourmet popcorn keeps customers informed using simple Facebook posts

Who: Sweet Poppin's has a flair for gourmet popcorn of all flavors. It makes over 30 gourmet flavored, chocolate-covered combinations sold in its Kokomo, Indiana, retail store as well as retailers in multiple states.

What it did: Sweet Poppin's founder Tashia Johnson uses her Facebook posts to share customer news and happenings to her loyal Sweet Poppin's followers as well as with well-wishers, family, and friends.

The results: Tashia found that her engagement on Facebook has encouraged new sales outside of her Kokomo base of operations. "It's helped me spread the word about my product," she said. "I can't pay for that type of advertising."

How TicketLeap sells more tickets through Facebook

Who: TicketLeap is a Philadelphia-based ticketing platform that enables event organizers to sell tickets quickly, track sales in real time, and get people talking about events from one unified system (see Figure 11.9). TicketLeap also allows ticket buyers to share where they're going through social media and see who else is attending events.

11.9 TicketLeap took the time to develop a very interactive Facebook Page to get fans and keep them engaged.

What it did: TicketLeap used Facebook as a key tool in increasing awareness of its services and promoting ticket sales (see Figure 11.10). TicketLeap's platform is deeply integrated with Facebook, which helps event organizers sell more tickets. Ticket buyers can opt in to post an "I'm going to X event" announcement to their Facebook Timeline which shows up on their friends' News Feeds and helps turn buyers into promoters or evangelists. In addition, from any event page, ticket buyers can invite their Facebook friends to events and opt in to post comments about the event directly to Facebook. TicketLeap has found that these social tools resulted in seven times more ticket sales, which TicketLeap attributes to the social nature of Facebook and live events. Ticket buyers can also register for TicketLeap events using Facebook Connect, a simplified way to log in to the site using their Facebook login credentials and information.

11.10 Linking back to its Facebook Page on blog posts and using tools like Facepile to authenticate users helped bring new fans to the TicketLeap fan Page.

The results: TicketLeap's incorporation of Open Graph led to large incremental sales. The decision also provided an analytic opportunity for the business, enabling it to determine the number of shares that lead to increments in ticket sales.

How Framework Media Strategies keeps customers informed with likes and shares

Who: Framework Media Strategies is an integrated communications team serving New Jersey-based clients with social media creation and management, public and media relations, and creative design.

What it did: According to owner Jeremiah Sullivan, Framework Management Strategies mostly relies on the plug-in features. "The tools we use most are the like and share and tagging functions that Facebook currently offers. All have proven to be valuable tools in our efforts to keep ourselves informed, as well as share our content (or viable content that relates directly to our business or clients) with new, yet interested eyes."

The results: The company's most successful use of Facebook tools has been strategically leveraging the like, share, and tagging functions to identify and engage elements of target audiences and raise general awareness of its content.

How the organic body care company Motherlove grows with Facebook

Motherlove Herbal Company (www.motherlove.com) manufactures best-in-industry organic body care products and herbal supplements for pregnancy, breast-feeding, childbirth, and baby care. It serves two niche markets — one for organic body care and baby products, and another for its best-selling breast-feeding supplements used by mothers who have low milk supply.

Because reaching any niche customer takes extra effort and because consumer education is key in increasing sales, Motherlove decided in 2010 to focus its marketing and advertising efforts in social media where it could build a community, converse with customers, and support other like-minded communities.

Educating mothers

Motherlove was founded 22 years ago by Kathryn Higgins, who saw the need for specialized herbal products for pregnancy, childbirth, and breast-feeding. The first company of its kind, Motherlove has always refused to accept the status quo, and its products, packaging, ingredients, business practices, and culture all reflect its commitment to quality and safety as well as a love for the earth.

But 22-year histories don't communicate themselves, and the organic marketplace is more crowded than ever. To reach new moms who are hungry for information about holistic products or have difficulty breast-feeding, Motherlove decided to focus on education first.

Content curation became the cornerstone of its social media approach. Using its Facebook Page, blog, and podcasts, as well as guest posts on other blogs, Motherlove created an online community that understood and valued its commitment to organic ingredients and sustainable practices (see Figure 11.11).

11.11 Motherlove Herbal Company used Facebook to build a community where it could educate fans and customers and answer their questions about breast-feeding and the holistic products it offers.

Motherlove started using Twitter after Facebook and now regularly participates in Twitter parties that provide real-time information. Most recently, Motherlove cosponsored the World's Largest Breastfeeding Twitter party (#BigBFParty).

Short-term customers

A significant challenge to any pregnancy-based company is the short life cycle of the consumer. Women are only pregnant for nine months, and they might not realize they are pregnant for two or more of those months. Women don't breast-feed forever, either, so the average customer only buys Motherlove products for a short window of time, perhaps several times as they continue to have children.

Because women don't immediately seek out products to help them with childbirth or breast-feeding upon becoming pregnant, Motherlove tries to form a connection with the women the very first time they hear about the brand. Motherlove has found social media well suited for forming that connection while educating the consumer and conveying Motherlove as the 22–year-old trusted resource.

Motherlove performed extensive testing as its first phase of social media adoption. It wanted to be confident that it was giving women the information they needed and wanted, and it was important to package that information correctly.

 Unlike most brands, Motherlove doesn't offer samples, discounts, coupons, or freebies. In fact, the company only offers a discount twice a year (World Breastfeeding Week and Mother's Day). That's a big departure from conventional Facebook Page building wisdom, but recent studies have shown that Motherlove's method works better in the long term.

The Motherlove team believes Facebook fans like its Page for four top reasons. First, because it is a community of like-minded breast-feeding advocates, many of whom have struggled to breast-feed or are still struggling. This is different from other breast-feeding communities where a large percentage of moms have either breast-fed easily or are not breast-feeding after returning to the workplace. Mothers also like the Page because they are looking for support or information in real time, as well as customer support and questions about the products. Finally, retailers and breast-feeding experts like the Page for information and to show support for the brand and the women using the products.

Advertising on Facebook

Motherlove uses Facebook ads to promote the Page and let new moms know it's there as a resource. It regularly tests all varieties of ads to see what works best for the specific product or content, and it changes the ads regularly. Promoted content is written by licensed breast-feeding experts.

Facebook ads are targeted to reach women interested in breast-feeding or buying organic body care products for pregnancy and childbirth. Using a variety of ads at different price ranges and targets allows Motherlove to keep a small daily budget (between $5 and $10) constantly display their advertisement. Motherlove also charts Facebook ad data to better understand what messages resonate with its fans. See Chapter 4 for more information on advertising on Facebook.

Motherlove advertises on websites with active Facebook communities and participates in Facebook chats with other brands. The focus is not on sales or even Motherlove products, but on educating consumers about why they might be struggling with low milk supply and helping all moms meet their breast-feeding goals. The promotion of breast-feeding as the normal way to feed a baby is central to every marketing outreach.

Building a community

Because moms who breast-feed are usually part of at least one online community where they share tips and information, Motherlove supports key communities and information sources. Sponsored Facebook chats, where Motherlove sponsors an independent breast-feeding expert to answer questions for community members about breast-feeding challenges are central to Motherlove's strategy of building a vibrant and supportive community for all moms, regardless of their breast-feeding goals.

End result: word of mouth

Rather than push sales via discounts, calls to action, or other direct methods, Motherlove has focused on using social media to educate consumers and breast-feeding experts about its products and support communities where moms share information. The result has been a groundswell of brand awareness and word of mouth from moms who have used the products. Recommendations of Motherlove products from mom to mom have increased at least tenfold. Sales have risen dramatically, and the number of new accounts each month has doubled despite the challenging economy.

The future

Motherlove's short-term social media plans include a new mobile-optimized website, mobile shopping cart, QR codes on labels, and a mobile product information website with videos and mobile-specific product information. Motherlove is also planning to join Google+.

 NOTE   *QR codes* are quick response bar codes that, once scanned, provide electronic information on a product.

Because Motherlove is a family legacy (as opposed to venture capital acquisition), marketing plans focus on long-term goals.

| Timeline | Info | Photos | Notes |

Resources

This appendix lists helpful resources for small business marketers.

Facebook News, Help, and Guidelines

Facebook for Business

https://www.facebook.com/business

Facebook Newsroom

http://newsroom.fb.com

Advertise on Facebook

https://www.facebook.com/advertising

Facebook Advertising Guidelines

https://www.facebook.com/ad_guidelines.php

Facebook Brand Permissions Center

https://www.facebook.com/brandpermissions/logos.php

Facebook Marketing

www.facebook.com/marketing

Preferred Marketing Developer Program

http://developers.facebook.com/preferredmarketingdevelopers

Facebook Video Calling
www.facebook.com/videocalling

Facebook Help Center
https://www.facebook.com/help

Promotion Applications

Wildfire
www.wildfireapp.com

North Social
http://northsocial.com

Woobox
http://woobox.com

Votigo
www.votigo.com

Strutta
www.strutta.com

Offerpop
http://offerpop.com

Social Plug-Ins

Facebook Social Plug-Ins
https://developers.facebook.com/docs/plugins

SexyBookmarks
http://sexybookmarks.shareaholic.com

Wibiya
http://wibiya.conduit.com

Analytic Tools

Hootsuite Pro
www.hootsuite.com

Crowdbooster
www.crowdbooster.com

PageLever
www.pagelever.com

Postling
www.postling.com

Google Analytics
www.google.com/analytics

Webtrends Social
www.webtrends.com

Radian6
www.radian6.com

Adobe Social
www.adobe.com/products/social.html

Video Streaming

Vpype
http://vpype.com

Ustream
www.ustream.tv/facebook

Justin.tv
www.facebook.com/Justintv

Brightcove
www.brightcove.com/en

Small Business Information

Smallbiztechnology.com
www.smallbiztechnology.com

Small Business Trends
http://smallbiztrends.com

Inc. Magazine
www.inc.com

AllBusiness.com
www.allbusiness.com

Entrepreneur.com
www.entrepreneur.com

OPEN Forum
www.openforum.com

Workshifting.com
www.workshifting.com

Blue Penguin Development Group

http://bluepenguindevelopment.com

ClickZ.com

www.clickz.com

The Small Business Web

www.thesmallbusinessweb.com

application (app) A program used for specific tasks. Apps as discussed in this book run within the Facebook site and usually enable you to connect with and share experiences with your friends. Most applications are built by third-party developers.

call to action The statement in the advertisement that tells the reader what action you want them to complete, such as "Buy 10 Cookies" or "Visit Our Store."

Check-in Deal A campaign requiring customers to indicate online that they are at a business or event in the real world in exchange for a special deal or similar incentive.

click-through rate (CTR) The rate, expressed as a percentage, in which someone clicks on an online advertisement.

cost per click (CPC) The cost paid per click for an online advertisement.

cost per thousand impressions (CPM) The cost of placing an advertisement on a site based on every 1,000 views it is assumed the ad will receive. For example, a website with 10,000 customers would sell a banner ad slot at this price times 10.

daily budget The maximum amount you would spend per day for your online advertising campaign.

decay The length of time your posts are on Facebook. The fresher the posts, the less decay.

destination URL The URL address for the page or website users are sent to once they click on your Facebook advertisement.

Event A Facebook item associated with an offline event, such as a wedding, celebration, rally, or simple get-together, that enables you to invite people to the event and to communicate with the attendees.

Facepile A plug-in that displays the Facebook profile pictures of users who have connected to your Page or signed up for your site.

friend (noun) A person on Facebook with whom you've agreed to share information.

friend (verb) To connect with another Facebook user by becoming that person's friend.

group A collection of people who share a common interest, such as a hobby, a passion, a cause, a protest, or just something fun or silly.

impressions The number of times your advertisement has been displayed on active web browsers.

landing page The destination page users arrive at in their browsers after clicking on an advertisement.

lifetime budget The total budget you allocate for the life of your advertisement.

like (verb) To indicate that you have a positive response toward a Facebook item or an item on a third-party website by clicking the "Like button" associated with it.

Like button An icon that appears on Facebook next to an item, such as a comment or Page, or on a third-party website that, when clicked, alerts the owner of the account the item is associated with and potentially those who view the item that you like that item.

Livestream A plug-in that enables Facebook users to view and potentially interact with an event in real time.

News Feed The automated collection of stories generated by the activities of your friends, the Pages you like, the groups you've joined, and the Events you're attending.

notification A message that Facebook sends to you whenever someone else does something on Facebook that relates to you, such as requesting to be your friend, accepting your friend request, commenting on a story, or sending you a message.

Page A special, nonpersonal Facebook profile designed to help businesses communicate with customers, organizations to communicate with users, and public figures or entities to communicate with fans.

Page design tool An editor you can use to create and edit the elements of your Facebook Page.

profile The collection of information about yourself that you've shared on Facebook, including your location, relationship status, interests, activities, education, work history, and contact info.

profile picture The picture (or logo) you use to represent your profile on your Facebook Page and personal Page.

pull media relations A strategy of having robust content and information wherein journalists seek you out for commentary and interviews.

push media relations A strategy of using press releases and other outreach to contact media and solicit their coverage of you.

share To add a friend's story to your Timeline or to share a link to another site on your profile, typically using the Share button.

social plug-in A website feature that enables you to interact with that website via your Facebook account and view items shared or liked by your friends. Examples include the Like button and a Facebook login.

Sponsored Stories Posts from your friends that an advertiser pays to have amplified so that there's a better chance of you seeing them.

Subscribe button A social plug-in that enables users to subscribe to your public updates on Facebook. This differs from the Like button in that it does not indicate a preference for your updates, Page, cause, and so on.

tag To identify a Facebook user in a photo, video, or place.

Timeline A showcase of status updates (including photos and anything else you might post) indexed by date. With the Timeline, you can scroll through these updates, post updates based on times in the past, and post status updates with dates in the past.

weight The value assigned to a post or other item on Facebook based on how much interaction, such as comments and likes, the item generates.

The Genius is in.

The new **iPad** PORTABLE GENIUS
978-1-118-17303-9

iPhone 5 PORTABLE GENIUS
978-1-118-35278-6

iPod & iTunes PORTABLE GENIUS — Third Edition
978-1-118-16628-4

OS X Mountain Lion PORTABLE GENIUS
978-1-118-40142-2

MacBook Pro PORTABLE GENIUS — Fourth Edition
978-1-118-36361-4

iPod touch PORTABLE GENIUS
978-1-118-06352-1

iMac PORTABLE GENIUS — Fourth Edition
978-1-118-42063-8

iOS App Development PORTABLE GENIUS
978-1-118-32989-4

MacBook Air PORTABLE GENIUS — Fourth Edition
978-1-118-37020-9

Aperture 3 PORTABLE GENIUS — Second Edition
978-1-118-27429-3

Microsoft **Office for Mac 2011** PORTABLE GENIUS
978-0-470-61019-0

Designed for easy access to tools and shortcuts, the Portable Genius series has all the information you need to maximize your Apple digital lifestyle. With a full-color interior and easy-to-navigate content, the Portable Genius series offers innovative tips and tricks as well as savvy advice that will save you time and increase your productivity.

Available in print and e-book formats.

WILEY

Guides to go.

Digital Field Guides are packed with essential information about your camera, plus great techniques for everyday shooting. Colorful and easily portable, they go where you go.

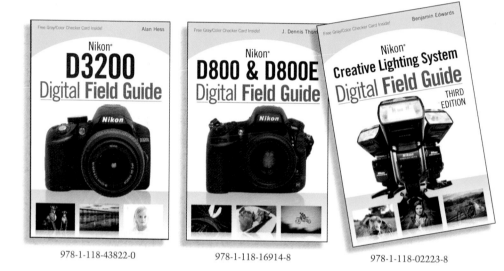

978-1-118-43822-0

978-1-118-16914-8

978-1-118-02223-8

978-1-118-16913-1

978-1-118-11289-2

978-1-118-16911-7

@ **Available in print and e-book formats.**

WILEY

Wiley is a registered trademark of John Wiley & Sons, Inc.